The
Church in the
Workplace

C. PETER WAGNER

Regal

From Gospel Light
Ventura, California, U.S.A.

PUBLISHED BY REGAL BOOKS
FROM GOSPEL LIGHT
VENTURA, CALIFORNIA, U.S.A.
PRINTED IN THE U.S.A.

Regal

Regal Books is a ministry of Gospel Light, a Christian publisher dedicated to serving the local church. We believe God's vision for Gospel Light is to provide church leaders with biblical, user-friendly materials that will help them evangelize, disciple and minister to children, youth and families.

It is our prayer that this Regal book will help you discover biblical truth for your own life and help you meet the needs of others. May God richly bless you.

For a free catalog of resources from Regal Books/Gospel Light, please call your Christian supplier or contact us at 1-800-4-GOSPEL *or* www.regalbooks.com.

Library of Congress Cataloging-in-Publication Data
Wagner, C. Peter.
  The church in the workplace / C. Peter Wagner.
    p. cm.
  Includes bibliographical references and index.
  ISBN 0-8307-3909-2 (hard cover)
  1. Work—Religious aspects—Christianity. I. Title.

BT738.5.W34 2006
261.8'5—dc22   2005034570

1   2   3   4   5   6   7   8   9   10   /   10   09   08   07   06

Rights for publishing this book in other languages are contracted by Gospel Light Worldwide, the international nonprofit ministry of Gospel Light. Gospel Light Worldwide also provides publishing and technical assistance to international publishers dedicated to producing Sunday School and Vacation Bible School curricula and books in the languages of the world. For additional information, visit www.gospellightworldwide.org; write to Gospel Light Worldwide, P.O. Box 3875, Ventura, CA 93006; or send an e-mail to info@gospellightworldwide.org.

with God materializes in the bedroom, so to speak. Intimacy is the key here. However, the same church also functions as an army, and the church's relationship to God in this case materializes not in the bedroom but in the throne room. There the divine Commander-in-Chief gives out the assignments for war. The cover of the book *Worship Warrior*, by Chuck Pierce and John Dickson, puts the two concepts together quite succinctly: "Ascending in Worship, Descending in War."

Every commander-in-chief expects that his or her army will not only fight the war but also go on to win it. If God gives us orders to transform the communities in which we live, we can legitimately expect that He will also give us the tools we need to accomplish His purpose. I believe that one of these tools is a clear understanding of the church in the workplace, and that is where we need to begin in this first chapter.

The Big Picture

The book of Revelation says several times, "He who has an ear, let him hear what the Spirit says to the churches" (Rev. 2:7,11,17,29; 3:6,13,22). While Christ spoke this during His revelation to the apostle John, I believe that its truth is applicable today as well.

In order to understand the significance of this Scripture, there are a couple of things to notice about it. First, the tense of the verb "says" is present, not past. There are many important things that the Holy Spirit *said* (past tense) to the churches, starting with the Bible itself.

At the same time, I believe just as strongly that the Holy Spirit did not stop speaking after the Bible was written and the canon of Scripture was established. The Spirit continues to speak, and God's people need to listen attentively. Parents need to know what the Spirit is saying to their families; teachers need to know what the Spirit is saying to their pupils; corporate executives need to know what the Spirit is saying to their companies; pastors need to know what the Spirit is saying to their church; believers on the city council need to know what the Spirit is saying to their community; and so on.

Contrary to what some people might think, however, it is not the responsibility of all believers, nor even of church pastors, to hear directly what the Spirit is saying to the *churches* (plural). Apostles are the ones who have been given the primary responsibility of hearing what the Spirit is saying to the churches. Those who provide apostolic leadership to a number of churches need to hear what the Spirit is saying to those churches under their apostolic covering. Likewise, those who have more of a horizontal jurisdiction need to hear what the Spirit is saying on an even broader basis.

True to my personal apostolic calling over the years, I have found myself developing the boldness (I hope it's not arrogance) to say that I am quite sure I am hearing a major global word from the Spirit. I imagine that I would not be as bold if I were the only one hearing this, but fortunately I am not the only one. Numbers of other leaders who also hear from God are now saying the same or similar things, providing further confirmation.

What is this word from the Spirit? *"Social transformation!"*

In a later chapter, I explain that the biblical rationale for the church, in all of its forms, is to aggressively seek to take dominion of the society in which we live. Meanwhile, in order to see the big picture, consider the following graphic.

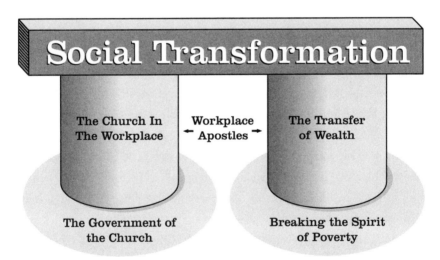

Social transformation is standing on two pillars: the church in the workplace and the transfer of wealth. Without both of them, we will not see our cities transformed. The pillar of the church in the workplace arises from the foundation of the biblical government of the church, and

Contents

PART 1
One Church but Two Operations

PART 2
The Two Rule Books

the pillar of the transfer of wealth arises from the foundation of breaking the spirit of poverty. Finally, the ongoing, dynamic linkage between the two pillars is provided by workplace apostles.

I am fully aware that the preceding paragraph contains much terminology that will be unfamiliar to many readers. However, my objective is to explain every one of the components of this graphic in such detail as we move through this book that it will end up making good sense. If I accomplish this purpose, I believe that we will all be hearing a very important thing that the Spirit is saying to the churches in this hour.

A Major Paradigm Shift

What I am suggesting is not some minor fine-tuning of what we have traditionally assumed. It is a major change that has been building for some time. I can testify, for example, that it demanded a radical change in my own thinking. For years I had been aware of the teaching on marketplace ministry that was emerging, and I had a favorable disposition toward it. But I had planned on keeping it at arm's length, letting others carry this particular ball, while I continued going about doing what I considered to be more important things. The change began when my friends Dennis and Megan Doyle of Minneapolis invited me to speak on marketplace ministry at a gathering of Nehemiah Partners in June 2001. My first inclination was to politely decline the invitation, but God surprised me with as clear a word as I have received from Him: "My son, I want you to pay strict attention to the church in the workplace."[1]

From that point on, it was no longer a matter of preference on my part; it was a matter of obedience. So I prepared a talk for Nehemiah Partners. The content of the talk was not particularly memorable, but the occasion was. It marked the beginning of my paradigm shift. At that point, I began to see things about believers in the marketplace that I had never seen before.

Not knowing much about this new assignment that God had given me, I, being a professional scholar, did what scholars usually do. I began to purchase and read all the books I could find on the subject at hand. At this writing, I now have purchased and read more than 100 books on the faith-at-work movement. I am amazed at how much the Holy Spirit has been revealing to so many people the tremendous power for social transformation that has been locked up in the church in the workplace.

What is a paradigm shift? A paradigm is simply a mental grid through which we interpret certain aspects of reality that come to our attention. We all know that two people can arrive at vastly different conclusions after processing exactly the same facts. That is because they have different paradigms. So a paradigm shift involves making changes in our mental grids. This will be necessary for most of us when we begin to hear what the Spirit is saying about the different components of the social-transformation graphic.

Notice that, because a paradigm is a mental grid, the central issue is how we *think*. This is what Paul had in mind when he wrote Romans 12:2: "Do not be conformed to this world, but be transformed by the renewing of your mind." Some important things in life require a change of heart. But a paradigm shift requires a renewing of the mind. We can be transformed if we begin to think properly.

What Happens in a Paradigm Shift?

What happens in a paradigm shift? Inevitably, we get pulled out of our comfort zones. We begin to realize that we need to make some adjustments to the way we had been thinking for a long time. This is easier for some than for others. Social science has studied this and has concluded that whenever a new innovation is introduced, some individuals are early adopters, some are middle adopters, some late adopters, and some are laggards who refuse to accept the innovation at all. To put it in plainer language, some people frequently find themselves ahead of the curve, while others settle for ending up behind the curve.

When the notion arises that the people of God in the workplace are, in fact, a legitimate form of the church, it proposes a significant innovation for most people. Consequently we should not be surprised if we find ourselves entering seasons of dialogue, debate and even heated disagreements. We are seeing a certain amount of conflict these days because leaders are being pushed to the boundaries of their comfort zones.

Although this is true, a major shift in thinking concerning the church in the workplace will eventually occur. Why do I say this? Because as I have already suggested, it is one of the things that the Spirit is currently saying to the churches. How long will the shift take? Who knows? It took the Sunday School movement (an equally radical paradigm shift some 200 years ago) at least a whole generation to become acceptable to the church at large. I don't think it will take quite that long for the church in the workplace to be accepted, but it won't happen overnight.

The Kingdom of God

In order to develop a mind-set that is receptive to the fact that the church exists in the marketplace, just as it also exists in the congregations that meet on Sundays, it is essential to understand the practical meaning of the term "the kingdom of God." True, every Bible reader is familiar with the phrase, but many have not yet grasped its broader implications. Consider Myles Monroe's testimony:

> I went to college and have a degree in theology, but there was not one class on the Kingdom. I read the four Gospels and it was the only thing that Jesus preached. That was a very strange contradiction to me. The Spirit of God has been speaking about the Kingdom for years, but we are finally listening and that's exciting to me. We will see the true impact of the Kingdom if we keep preaching it.[2]

One reason that some have not been listening, as Myles Monroe laments, is that they have imagined that the church and the kingdom of God are the same thing. Others have thought that the church is here now, while the kingdom of God is something that will come when the Lord returns. Both of these ideas are very common among believers today, but both are erroneous. If we hang on to either one, we will not be able to shift our paradigm and move with the current flow of the Holy Spirit.

The kingdom of God is not confined to the four walls of the local church. It never has been. It is much broader than that. Where, then, is the kingdom of God? How do we identify it? For a starter, the kingdom of God is not a kingdom of this world. It has no territorial boundaries. It does not issue passports. It cannot join the United Nations.

Still, the kingdom of God is not simply a metaphor or a figure of speech. It is tangible. It is not something that we are waiting for. It exists here on the earth right now. The kingdom of God is to be found wherever there are individuals who exalt Jesus Christ as their King. They recognize that Jesus is the King of kings and the Lord of lords and that all loyalty and obedience are due Him. This is what Jesus meant when He said, "The kingdom of God is within you" (Luke 17:21).

"Your Kingdom Come"

It is God's desire that the values, the blessings and the prosperity of the kingdom of God penetrate all areas of society. This was foremost in Jesus' mind when He was on Earth. For example, think of what He said to His disciples when they asked Him to teach them to pray. He responded with what we now call the Lord's Prayer. It is interesting to note that Jesus gave His disciples this prayer not once, but twice. The two instances, as recorded in Matthew and Luke, occurred a year and a half apart. Both times Jesus taught them to pray, "Your kingdom come. Your will be done on earth as it is in heaven" (Matt. 6:10; Luke 11:2).

The only way that our society and the communities in which we live are going to become characterized by the values of the kingdom of God is through believers like you and me. The kingdom of God is within us, and we are the ones responsible for advancing it wherever we live and minister. As I have said, the church's divine assignment is nothing short of transforming society. We, of course, cannot do it alone. We need each other, just as every member of a body needs every other member to function at the optimum level. That's why we are called the Body of Christ.

On the whole, as the Body of Christ, we've connected with each other fairly well in our local congregations. We've also made considerable progress in promoting unity among the pastors and churches in our cities. But we have been weak in connecting with the church, our fellow believers, in the workplace.

Chapter 1

The Church in
the Workplace

This is a book on the church in the workplace. I hope it will help you understand that the true church of Jesus Christ does not only take the form that usually comes to mind when we hear the word "church," namely, congregations of believers that meet together for worship on Sundays (as well as for other congregational activities), but that this same true church also takes the form of the dispersion of believers out in the workplace the other six days of the week.

The Church: Both a Bride and an Army

Understanding those two forms of one church is a necessary starting point, but not the finishing point, of this book. The finishing point is much broader. I hope that it will bring us to the place where we will be doing our part to glorify God through the actual transformation of society itself. True, there are legitimate ways of thinking of the church as an end in itself, such as seeing the church as the Bride of Christ. But there are other equally legitimate ways of thinking of the church. One of them, for example, is characterizing the church as the army of God. In this scenario, the church becomes a means toward an end, not an end in itself. The church moves out onto the battlefield, marshaled against the forces of the enemy, with the divine assignment to retake the dominion of society, which Satan usurped from Adam.

This book leans toward the battlefield approach. By saying this, I don't want to be misunderstood as trivializing the fact that the church is also the Bride. It certainly is, and as such, the church's relationship

Part 1

One Church but
Two Operations

The Church Versus the World

One of the reasons for this weakness has been a common mind-set of the old paradigm, namely, the notion that the world is our enemy. True, Satan uses the world and the flesh to combat us in every way. However, we should not allow this to be an excuse to abandon the world. Jesus said that we are to be *in* the world, but not *of* it (see John 17:13-14). That is why we must renew our minds and no longer think of the local church as something against the marketplace.

Fortunately, this is changing. Much of the literature that I referred to previously is teaching how we should relate to the world positively, and increasing numbers of believers are agreeing with their responsibility to minister in the workplace. I like the way that Jack Graham of Prestonwood Baptist Church in Dallas, Texas, puts it: "Revival will come when we get the walls down between the church and the community."[3]

In the 1990s, many church leaders applied this axiom to the global-prayer movement with notable success. But now I see that it is equally important to apply it to apostolic ministry in the 2000s. The obvious reason for this is that God's people are out in the community most of the time. Think of it this way: Believers *live* in the marketplace; they *visit* their local congregations only once or twice a week.

I realize that some people will have difficulty with a thought like that. And I think that I can identify the major reason why. It is because we, particularly those of us in the Western world, live with a mind-set that has been molded by Greek (or Greco-Roman) thinking. This is extremely important, so let me try to explain what I mean.

The Greek Mind-set of Dualism

Most of us who were born in the United States and who can trace our lineage back to Western Europe or the British Isles have had our minds molded, to a large extent, by Greek philosophy. We may not have studied much philosophy in school, but the name Plato, and the fact that he had a great deal to do with the way we think, is common knowledge. Of course Plato was not the only Greek philosopher who influenced subsequent Western civilization, but he is arguably the most famous.

Plato has gone down in history as a chief protagonist of what is called dualism. According to him, the world is divided into two levels. John Beckett, a businessman and one of the chief leaders of today's church in the workplace, describes these levels in his book *Loving Monday*:

> [Plato] sought to identify unchanging universal truths, placing them in the higher of two distinct realms. The upper level he called "form," consisting of eternal ideas. The lower level he called "matter." The lower realm was temporal and physical. Plato's primary interest lay in the higher form. He deemed it superior to the temporary and imperfect world of matter.[4]

Beckett, whose purpose in his book is to help us see that the work that most believers do between Sundays is a valid form of Christian ministry, goes on to write, "The rub comes when we see where Plato placed work and occupations. Where, indeed? In the lower realm."[5]

Why has this been a major obstacle to our appreciating the true validity of the church in the workplace? Here is the way one of our most respected marketplace leaders, Dennis Peacocke, explains it:

> Dualism has polluted evangelical Christianity in grievous ways. The marketplace was "carnal" because it dealt with "earthly things" like business and money. Adultery was properly viewed as sinful, but the worldly realm of economics was viewed, like politics, as some kind of "neutral zone" where Christianity had no real place trying to affect the system of economics, production, management, or distribution. Hence, no Christian ministry was possible in that realm.[6]

Where did the Greek philosophers get their information? From human ideas. They believed that humankind was supreme. That is why their philosophy is also called humanism or secular humanism.

The Hebrew Mind-set of Unity

The biblical way, the Hebrew way, of understanding life is quite different from Plato's. Humans are not the center of the Hebrew worldview; God is. Truth does not come from human reason; it comes from divine revelation. For the Hebrews, the only upper level of the world is God; all the rest, visible or invisible, is under God. James Thwaites explains it in this way:

> Platonic thought believes there is a spiritual realm that is separate and distinct from the natural/created realm. The Hebrews, on the other hand, saw the divine presence and word in, through, and over all things of the present creation. The Hebrews saw the heaven of God, his throne, existing over all of their life and work in the present age.[7]

In other words, while Plato saw work as something separate from and inferior to the purity of the spiritual realm, Hebrews see both the spiritual and the natural (including work) realms as one entity under the hand of God.

The conclusion that can be derived from the Hebrew perspective is that our work is a form of ministry. It is as sacred as singing in the choir. I know that this can be hard to agree with at first, because we have been programmed with the Greek mind-set. But the more we can switch our paradigm to the Hebrew mind-set, the better we will understand the church in the workplace.

The Nuclear Church and the Extended Church

Until this point I have frequently affirmed that there is a church in the workplace, but I have not as yet addressed the issue from a biblical perspective. The biblical word translated as "church" is *ekklesia* (sometimes spelled *ecclesia*). The root meaning of "ekklesia" in the original Greek is simply "the people of God." The New Testament uses this word in two different ways. Sometimes it refers to the people of God gathered together in congregations. That is our traditional idea of the local church. But other times it means believers in general, wherever they might find themselves. Both are the true church.

David Oliver and James Thwaites, in their book *Church That Works*, provide a helpful description of the different forms that the church takes. They write:

> Our theology of the church has caused us to emphasize this gathering aspect over every other element the word *ekklesia* might contain. For example, in Ephesians the word *ekklesia* is never used in relation to the gathering. . . . Certainly, the household gatherings of the saints are gatherings of the church, but we need to understand that it is not the gathering that makes them the church. They are the church and so when they gather they gather as that church.[8]

We must agree that the church takes on two forms. One is the gathering of believers in local church congregations each Sunday. The other is the scattered body of believers throughout the workplace the other six days of the week. They are the same people, namely, the people of God. From the Hebrew perspective, they are one church, living in harmony, not opposing or competing with each other. However, the way the church functions when it is gathered is quite different from the way it functions when it is scattered. It is like a football team that behaves one way out on the playing field and another way in the locker room. But I'll discuss the church's differences in function in later chapters.

What is the best terminology to describe these two forms of the church? In my opinion, the terms "church and world," "church and marketplace," "priests and kings," "church and Kingdom" and "pulpit and marketplace" all reflect to one degree or another the Greek way of thinking. They maintain the distinction between the sacred and the secular, though both forms are actually the church. I like "gathered church and scattered church" better, because the term signifies that both forms are the church. However, I have concluded that the best terminology of all is "nuclear church and extended church," which builds on the commonly accepted sociological concepts of the nuclear family and the extended family.

Sociologically, the nuclear family consists of mother and father and children and those who live under the same roof. The extended family consists of the nuclear family along with grandparents, grandchildren, in-laws, aunts, uncles, cousins and so on. Both are family, but they are two different forms of the same family.

To follow this analogy, I have chosen "extended church" to refer to the church in the workplace.

Ministry in the Extended Church

Until recently I was so much of a traditionalist that I wrote in some of my books that all true ministry needed to be congregationally based. I thought that the whole church was only the nuclear church. It had not entered my mind that another form of the true church could be the extended church. I even went so far as to teach that spiritual gifts were given to use only in the nuclear church.

I mention this because I want to empathize with those who have not yet gone through the paradigm shift that I am advocating in this book. If you are one of them, be assured that I understand where you are coming from. But I also want to encourage you to begin to stretch your ideas of church and ministry. Let's live in the present, not in the past.

What God's people (the ekklesia) do in the extended church can be considered ministry just as much as leading a small group, teaching Sunday School, greeting those who come to church on Sunday, praying for the sick after church services and even pastoring the church. I will go into this in a lot more detail later on in the book, but for now, let me help ease some readers through the paradigm shift by ending with a thought that will be new to many, namely, that *work is sacred.*

Work Is Sacred

Once again, let's try to think more like Hebrews. Work is part of God's original design for the human race. According to Genesis 2:15, when God put Adam and Eve in the Garden of Eden, He put them there to work the garden. This is a far cry from Plato's teaching that work was part of a physical realm that was inferior to a spiritual realm. Work is of God; it is just as spiritual or as sacred as any other part of God's original creation.

I like the way that Robert Tamasy puts it:

> Work is sacred. It was ordained by God from the beginning, before the fall of man. After the fall, it just got rougher, frustrating, exhausting, sometimes even boring. But work pursued with excellence and integrity is still pleasing to God, a way of honoring Him by serving in the unique ways He has equipped us.[9]

Now, let's kick this up another notch. Work can even be regarded as a form of worship. I know that some who read this will suspect that I may be going too far, but first consider what Mark Greene says about this:

> Work is ordained by God. And it should be dedicated to God.... The Hebrew word for work is *avodah*, the same as the word for worship. "Service" captures the flavour best. Work is a seven-letter word—service—to God and people. And though I would lose my job if I built a theology on the basis of that observation alone, we can see elsewhere in scripture that work is a part of "everything" we do "to the glory of God." For God, work is part of our worship. It is part of our service to him.[10]

The other day in church I was singing Matt Redman's song "Let Everything That Has Breath." When we came to the line "I will worship You with every breath," I got to thinking about the premise behind that line. Part of worship is obviously singing songs like this one in church on Sunday, no question. However, that is not all worship is. If we really believe that we can worship God with every breath, wouldn't we be worshiping God with every breath at work? I can remember how relieved I was when the Holy Spirit gave me this thought. Why? Because, to be honest, I enjoy working even more than I enjoy singing. And it gives me hope that there will be work in heaven as well as times of singing new songs as we gather around the throne of the Lamb. The thought of sitting around and playing a harp for all of eternity has never been that appealing.

I love the way that Gregory Pierce sums it up in his book *spirituality @work*:

> The spirituality of work is a disciplined attempt to align ourselves and our environment with God and to incarnate God's spirit in the world through all the effort (paid and unpaid) we exert to make the world a better place, a little closer to the way God would have things.[11]

Yes, there is a church in the workplace—we are that church—and what we do in the workplace is just as much ministry, service to God and even worship as what we do on Sunday in our local church.

Chapter 2

Apostles in the Workplace

The church, as we would all agree, is not a human institution. The church was designed by the eternal God and instituted by Jesus when He came to Earth. This is a very important assumption because, throughout history, church leaders have tended to deviate from God's blueprint quite radically. The rest of this chapter profiles God's design for the church.

The Design for Building the Church

In Matthew 16, Jesus mentioned the church to His disciples for the first time. At that point, He had been with them for a year and a half. It took that long for the disciples to become thoroughly convinced that Jesus was, indeed, the Messiah that the Jewish people had been waiting for. Peter expressed that for the group when he said to Jesus, "You are the Christ [in Hebrew, "Messiah"], the Son of the living God" (Matt. 16:16). In response, Jesus said, "On this rock I will build My church" (v.18). This was the first time Jesus ever mentioned the word "church." He finally could tell them why He had come, because they now knew for sure who He was.

Jesus declared not only that He would build His church here on Earth but also how it would be built. When He first began to reveal His future role, it caused quite a fuss among the disciples. They had probably assumed that Jesus would be with them forever and that He would lead them as a team to build the church. But, no, that was not to be. The same day that Jesus told His disciples that He had come to build His church, He also revealed that He would soon be leaving them. The immediate implication was that they would be doing it on their own. Peter didn't like that idea at all, and he made the serious mistake of getting into an argument with the Master. The reason we know it was quite a fuss is that Jesus had to use some of His strongest language in correcting Peter: "Get behind Me, Satan!" (Matt. 16:23).

Later, when things calmed down, Jesus explained to His disciples why He needed to leave and why it would even be to their advantage: "If I do not go away, the Helper will not come to you; but if I depart, I will send Him to you" (John 16:7). The Helper, of course, is the Holy Spirit. This establishes an important theological axiom that many have not seen as clearly as they might: *For the purposes of building the church, the immediate presence of the Third Person of the Trinity is more important than the immediate presence of the Second Person of the Trinity.*

Power from on High

That is why Jesus told His disciples that when He left them, they should not go out and start evangelizing immediately. Even though they had received three years of the highest-quality training from the Master Himself, they were not ready to start building the church. The first thing they were supposed to do was to "tarry in the city of Jerusalem until [they were] endued with power from on high" (Luke 24:49). Without the power of the Holy Spirit, their best efforts, even based on impeccable training, would be fruitless.

In fact, Jesus reiterated this in the very last words He spoke here on Earth. After He was crucified and raised from the dead, He spent 40 more days with His disciples. The last thing He said to them was this: "But you shall receive power when the Holy Spirit has come upon you; and you shall be witnesses to Me in Jerusalem, and in all Judea and Samaria, and to the end of the earth" (Acts 1:8). Immediately, He was taken up into the clouds and He was gone. He is now at the right hand of the Father making intercession for those of us whom He left behind to build His church.

Fortunately, the disciples obeyed Jesus and went to Jerusalem, where they received the Holy Spirit on the day of Pentecost. Jesus' disciples, empowered by the Holy Spirit, have been building His church ever since.

The Government of the Church

But that was not all that happened on the day that Jesus ascended into heaven. Jesus also revealed the government of the church that He had instituted. Since the church is not a human institution but a divinely designed institution, it is essential that we understand and accept at face value what Jesus did. We do not get these important details from Acts, but rather from what God revealed through Paul in his letter to the Ephesians.

Paul brings us back to that same ascension day when he writes, "When [Christ] ascended on high, He led captivity captive, and gave gifts to men" (Eph. 4:8). On the day Jesus ascended, He left behind men and women who had become His disciples and whom He had endowed with spiritual gifts. They were the ones who would represent Him from then on, as the Body of Christ, and through them Jesus would build His church, as He said He would.

Paul goes on to tell us that Jesus gave these gifted men and women to the church to work on two levels. Let's call these levels the governmental level and the ministry level, for want of better terms. Paul describes Christ's establishing the governmental level like this: "He Himself gave some to be apostles, some prophets, some evangelists, and some pastors and teachers" (Eph. 4:11). The chief responsibility of these church leaders is "to equip the saints for the work of ministry for the edifying [or "building"] of the body of Christ" (v. 12). This takes us to the second level, the ministry level, which is supposed to be done by the saints in general under the equipping ministry of the first five types of leaders.

Allow me to pause a moment and say how surprised I am that most of the church has not understood the fivefold leadership of the church until fairly recently. When I went to seminary, I was taught that we need evangelists, pastors and teachers in the church today, but the ministry of apostles and prophets had supposedly been discontinued after the first century or so. However, since I started to take this passage in

Ephesians 4 literally a few years ago, I began to realize how flawed that teaching really was. The very same chapter of Scripture goes on to tell us how long we need all five: "Till we all come to the unity of the faith, . . . to a perfect man, to the measure of the stature of the fullness of Christ" (Eph. 4:13). No one I know would claim that we have yet arrived there, so I would conclude that we still need apostles and prophets as well as evangelists, pastors and teachers.

The Church's Foundation

Equipping the saints is one thing, but some will say that is not necessarily governing. True, so let's go back a couple of chapters to Ephesians 2:20, where Paul describes the church as the "household of God." He explains that the church is "built on the foundation of the apostles and prophets, Jesus Christ Himself being the chief corner stone" (v. 20). In a broad theological sense, Jesus is, of course, the foundation of the church because, as I have discussed, He came to Earth in order to institute it. However, according to this Scripture, after He ascended and sent the Holy Spirit, He left the nuts and bolts of building the church to the leadership of apostles and prophets. Jesus is still there, but as the cornerstone, not as the foundation itself. The cornerstone holds the foundation together, but the foundation itself is clearly apostles and prophets.

If any doubts remain as to the divine order of leadership in the church, we need only to go to the most detailed chapter on spiritual gifts in the Bible, namely, 1 Corinthians 12. There the gift of apostle is listed along with many other spiritual gifts. The governmental order comes in verse 28: "God has appointed these in the church: first apostles, second prophets, third teachers, after that miracles, then gifts of healings, helps, administrations, varieties of tongues." Churches that fail to recognize the position of apostles and prophets, not in a hierarchy but in a divine order, cannot expect to be everything that God originally designed them to be.

The title of this chapter is "Apostles in the Workplace." I have taken time at the outset to explain, as concisely as I am able, the place that apostles have in the church in general. Unless we are convinced that there are such things as apostles and that apostles are active today, we cannot begin to understand how they are supposed to function in the workplace.

Fortunately, much of the Body of Christ has begun to recognize the leadership of apostles and prophets, although it has taken awhile for things to get in order. I personally believe that God started doing a new thing, at least in our churches here in North America, after World War II, around the middle of the last century. The biblical government of the church had been out of place for so long that the process of reestablishing the government of the church took many years; and at the beginning, some of it was a bit messy.

The Second Apostolic Age

Soon after World War II, a restoration stream called the Latter Rain arose, along with the Discipling Movement, or the Shepherding Movement. The Latter Rain advocated the contemporary offices of apostle and prophet, but some of the leaders became divisive, veering off course, and the movement lost strength. The Discipling Movement eventually imploded because of a misunderstanding of authority and submission, with some of its founding leaders publicly apologizing for the movement. Many of these leaders made their share of mistakes, but God nevertheless used them as significant forerunners.

During the 1980s, the Spirit began speaking to the churches once again about the gift of prophecy and the office of prophet. During the 1990s, the gift and office of apostle began to be better understood and appreciated. What I have called the New Apostolic Reformation began to gain definition and recognition, and by the end of the century it was listed as the largest segment of the worldwide church outside of Catholicism and the fastest growing of all.[1]

The First Apostolic Age, which characterized the first century or two of Christianity, recognized the gifts and offices of apostle and prophet as the foundation of the church. This biblical church government subsequently was neglected and fell into disuse until around the beginning of the twenty-first century, which I estimate marks the emergence of what could be called the Second Apostolic Age.[2]

The upshot of this is that we are currently living in the time of the most radical change in the form of the church's leadership since the Protestant Reformation, and the implications of this are huge when we begin to hear what the Spirit is saying to the churches about the kingdom of God and the transformation of society.

Spiritual Authority

Of all the changes involved with the emergence of the New Apostolic Reformation, the most radical of all is the following: *the recognition of the amount of spiritual authority delegated by the Holy Spirit to individuals.* Previously, church authority, whether in local congregations or in denominational structures, invariably rested on groups, not on individuals. The groups were called church councils, sessions, vestries, presbyteries, conferences, synods, deacon boards, annual conventions, districts, cabinets, general councils, or what have you. With the exception of those leaders who stepped out of their traditional molds and founded entire new movements, individuals were not to be trusted to make final decisions.

However, this is not true of churches that find themselves as part of the New Apostolic Reformation. The acceptance of individuals who are entrusted with a great deal of spiritual authority plays out on two levels in today's apostolic movement:

- On the local level, the pastor is the leader of the church; he's not an employee.
- On the translocal level, the apostle's leadership is welcomed and appreciated by the churches and ministries that voluntarily place themselves under the spiritual covering of the apostle.

What, then, is an apostle? An apostle is a Christian leader who is gifted, taught, commissioned and sent by God with the authority to establish the foundational government of the church within an assigned sphere of ministry by hearing what the Spirit is saying to the churches and by setting things in order, accordingly, for the growth and maturity of the church. I will explain this definition in greater detail as we continue.

Apostles in the Extended Church?

If God has given apostles to the church today, it follows that He has given them to both forms that the church takes, namely, the nuclear church and the extended church. If the church in the workplace is part of the legitimate church (in the previous chapter I argued strongly that it is), it will certainly have a biblical foundation. That foundation, of course, is apostles and prophets (see Eph. 2:20).

Earlier in this chapter, I mentioned that during the 1990s, the gift and office of apostle began to be better understood. Since then, a tremendous amount of quality literature has been coming from leaders of the New Apostolic Reformation. At this writing I have 71 books on apostolic ministry in my personal library, and I am sure that there are many more out there. However, almost all of them deal with apostles and apostolic ministry in the *nuclear* church, not in the *extended* church. One notable exception is Bill Hamon's book *The Day of the Saints*. In it, Hamon dedicates no fewer than 82 pages to the ministry of not only apostles but also prophets, evangelists, pastors and teachers, all in the workplace. Two others are Rich Marshall's *God@Work, Volume 2,* and Os Hillman's *The 9 to 5 Window*.

Even after I began writing on apostles some years ago, it took me quite awhile to convince myself that God had assigned certain apostles to ministry in the workplace. One of the things that had hindered me was the lack of a convincing, biblical role model. Paul was my role model of an apostle in the nuclear church, but I had none in the extended church. It was back in 2001, only after I heard God tell me to pay attention to the church in the workplace and I agreed to obey, that He suddenly opened my eyes to the obvious. Luke was a workplace apostle. Why hadn't I seen that before? And then Lydia entered the picture as well.

Luke and Lydia as Workplace Apostles

When I researched and wrote my commentary on the book of Acts, *Acts of the Holy Spirit,* back in 1994, I began to suspect that Luke could well have married Lydia. Let me hasten to say that none of the classic commentaries on Acts that I know about suggests this, so I must admit that my hypothesis may be a bit on the speculative side. Even so, let me summarize my rationale.

Luke was a workplace person, a physician (see Col. 4:14). Let's use our imaginations. As many physicians would be, he was more than likely well-educated, cultured, well-traveled, rich, handsome and single. Luke was a Gentile God-fearer and also the author of the book of Acts.

At one point in Acts, Paul, Silas and Timothy embark on a missionary journey, and they end up in Troas. There Paul receives the "Macedonian vision," by which God directs him to Philippi, the major city of Macedonia (see Acts 16:9-10). When they depart from Troas to Macedonia, the narrative in the book of Acts suddenly changes from third person ("they") to first person ("we"), indicating that Luke, the author, had joined the missionary team in Troas (see v. 11).

When the four missionaries arrive in Philippi, they locate a group of women who regularly conduct a prayer meeting by the river. One of them is Lydia, a seller of purple. The phrase "seller of purple" implies that she is an international businesswoman. She probably has an import-export business, which would make her very much involved in the marketplace. Let's use our imaginations again. As a businesswoman, she is more than likely well-educated, cultured, well-traveled, rich, beautiful and single. Lydia, like Luke, is also a Gentile God-fearer.

Extraordinary things happen in Philippi. The missionaries preach the Gospel, people are saved and healed and demons are cast out, so much so that the whole city goes into an uproar. Paul and Silas get thrown in prison, there is an earthquake, they are supernaturally released, the jailer is saved and a wonderful congregation of believers is planted. After all this happens, the last place we see the four missionaries is in Lydia's house (see Acts 16:40). Then, when they finally leave for Thessalonica, the narrative in the book of Acts changes back from "we" to "they," indicating that Luke stays there in the house of Lydia (see 17:1). I admit that I can't prove beyond any doubt that Luke and Lydia actually get married, but I can say, with some pardonable romantic enthusiasm, that it is not unlikely. These two marketplace people would become a vital part of the nucleus of that strong congregation in Philippi.

Luke's Apostolic Characteristics

If, as I am advocating, Luke is a prototype of a workplace apostle, what would some of his apostolic characteristics include?

Luke's foremost apostolic credential would be his divine anointing to write two books of the New Testament, the Gospel of Luke and the Acts of the Apostles. I have already mentioned that one of the responsibilities of an apostle is to hear what the Spirit is saying to the churches. Luke took hearing from God to the limits by writing under such a strong inspiration of the Spirit that his writings became canonized and considered the Word of God by the church in general. While subsequent apostles, such as those recognized as apostles today, will never write holy Scripture, what they do hear from God should nevertheless be taken very seriously by the churches.

Let's make note of the fact that Luke, an extended-church apostle, wrote inspired New Testament Scriptures on exactly the same level as the other New Testament authors, all of whom we would likely consider to be nuclear-church apostles. I point this out to defuse any notion that extended-church apostles are, somehow, junior apostles or not quite on as high a level as clergy-type, nuclear-church apostles.

A second apostolic credential for Luke would be the fact that he was a missionary and a church planter. I have already mentioned that Luke was on the missionary team that planted the church of Philippi. But that was not the only time he did missionary work, as we know from the other sections of Acts that were written in the first person "we." For example, Luke was with Paul on a trip from Philippi to Troas to Miletus (see Acts 20:5—21:17); he joined Paul on Paul's voyage from Jerusalem to Rome (see Acts 27:1—28:16); and quite probably he did other missionary work that he did not choose to record when he wrote Acts.

A third credential might be Luke's close, personal relationship with the apostle Paul. I surmise that they were best friends because Luke visited Paul twice when he was in prison in Rome. During his first jail term, Paul penned the letter to the Colossians, in which he wrote, "Luke the beloved physician and Demas greet you" (Col. 4:14). It would probably also be fair to assume that as a part of their relationship, Luke would have provided ongoing medical care for Paul. During Paul's second jail term, Paul wrote his second letter to Timothy. In chapter 4, he wrote, "Only Luke is with me" (2 Tim. 4:11), after lamenting that others, such as Demas, Crescens and Titus, had left him (see vv. 9-10).

A fourth indication that Luke was an active workplace apostle was his access to wealth. If, indeed, he and Lydia were married, she could have brought considerable wealth to the family, given the fact that her private house was large enough to accommodate the four missionaries while they were in Philippi. And since like attracts like, if Luke and Lydia were the leaders of the Philippian church, it could well have been that the upper class of Philippi was well-represented among the believers.

Paul's letter to the Philippians is essentially an extended thank-you for financial provisions. Paul was in prison when he wrote it, and Luke was in Philippi. In the letter, Paul addresses Luke as his "true companion" (Phil. 4:3; the *New King James Version* translates the title as "true yokefellow"). He reminisces about the time when "no church shared with me concerning giving and receiving but you only" (v. 15) when Paul had left Luke in Lydia's house and had gone on to Thessalonica; and he expresses joy that the church had again sent him money in prison; "your care for me has flourished again" (v. 10). Apparently, Paul had received a substantial amount of money from the Philippians, because he wrote, "I have all and abound" (v. 18).

Moving Beyond Finances

I need to make an important disclaimer here. While Luke, as a workplace apostle, provided financial support for the ministry of his friend Paul, his support of the nuclear church did not end there.

For too long a time, many nuclear-church leaders have expected that the principal role of their marketplace people, especially business leaders, was simply to provide the funding for their church-related programs. Megan Doyle, a prominent workplace leader who has thought these things through in a very practical way, writes:

Another finance-related area of division between the church and businesspeople occurs in the area of fund-raising. In this area it has often been pastors and ministry leaders who have hurt many businesspeople. Fund-raising for church and ministry definitely needs to occur with tact and sensitivity. The problem for businesspersons is when they are targeted for their money to the exclusion of anything else they have to offer—even to the exclusion of relationship. There are many businesspeople who believe their only purpose for the Kingdom of God is to provide funding. This leaves them frustrated and unfulfilled. The Christian businessperson can do much more than offer "provision for those with vision."[3]

Luke's relationship with Paul provides an outstanding example of a relationship between an extended-church apostle and the nuclear church. Luke was a provider of funds for a nuclear-church ministry, but at the same time he was a "true companion," a fellow missionary and an apostolic peer.

The Crucial Role of Extended-Church Apostles

When I suggested that Luke was an apostolic peer of Paul, only those who have made the paradigm shift that I am talking about will grasp the implications. For example, many pastors who have gone through seminary, passed ordination examinations and received a call to pastor a church would have a difficult time considering a lay member of their church, who happens to be a physician or whatever else, as a religious peer. At the root of that attitude is the assumption that the only true church is the nuclear church. However, once we recognize that the extended church is just as much the church as the nuclear church, our attitudes will begin to change.

We will then begin to recognize that for many of the purposes of God, such as the transformation of society, the apostolic role of workplace leaders will prove to be far more influential than that of nuclear-church apostles.

What do I mean?

When the people of God are gathered in their local churches on Sunday, the characteristics of a particular congregation or denomination or apostolic network are very important. The church might be Lutheran or Baptist or Word-Faith or Assemblies of God or Willow Creek or Presbyterian or what have you. However, on the other six days of the week, when God's people are in the workplace, those distinctions are not nearly as important. The most important thing out there is that they are believers and that they are brothers and sisters in Christ.

Most brothers and sisters in Christ out in the workplace realize that they are supposed to be salt and light. They are supposed to influence their workplace environment. They have heard it in sermons time and time again. Yet they feel frustrated. They wonder if they are spiritually impotent. They may have tried to be salt and light in their workplaces for 15 years, but nothing may have changed. In some instances, the atmosphere of their workplaces may be worse than before.

What is going on? Why haven't their small segments of society been changed or transformed? It is clearly the will of God that His kingdom comes to the workplace, but something is preventing it. What could that be?

It all has to do with government. Satan has a sophisticated government through which he is trying to control society, as I will explain in detail in the next chapter. Meanwhile, even though God's people are out there in the workplace, they have no government. Apostles are not yet setting things in order in most workplaces as they should be. Not many nuclear-church apostles could do this, one reason being that most of them represent just one denomination or apostolic network or megachurch, and the believers from other streams might not be inclined to follow them. However, extended-church apostles, when they are identified and recognized, would be the ones to establish the government of the church in the workplace. Once this happens, Satan will be in trouble!

The sooner we understand that there are extended-church apostles and the sooner we allow them to take their God-given place and respect them for doing it, the sooner we will make significant strides toward transforming society.

Characteristics of Workplace Apostles

It goes without saying that just as not every believer in the church is an apostle, neither is every believer in the workplace an apostle. The characteristics of nuclear-church apostles are fairly clear, but not the characteristics of extended-church apostles. Undoubtedly, there is a large degree of overlap between the two, but they are not the same.

However, the character traits of all apostles will be the same. Integrity, humility, holiness, godliness, respectability and blamelessness are essential to both. Both will meet the requirements of leadership that are listed in 1 Timothy 3:1-7. Both will have been given the gift of apostle (see 1 Cor. 12:28), and consequently they will know how to set things in order (see Titus 1:5).

Apostles are distinguished from other leaders, more than anything else, by their God-given authority. As I already mentioned, apostles have the authority to establish the foundational government of the church within an assigned sphere of ministry. The spheres of ministry within the workplace would include family, religion, business, government, education, arts and media. Each of these of course could be subdivided, but we need to be looking for apostles within each of the seven spheres. Perhaps a few workplace apostles could function in more than one of these spheres, but not many.

For example, Stephanie Klinzing is mayor of Elk River, Minnesota. She is a part of a broad-based movement, Pray Elk River, designed to bring social transformation to the city. Although the term "apostle" is not yet used, Klinzing is functioning with the authority of an apostle. Here is what she says:

> We have also discovered that I have spiritual authority in the city as well as civic authority. I have stood, in the spirit, against things that I believe God does not want in my city, and I have also opened, in the spirit, the city gates to things that I believe God wants in the city. This has had powerful results.[4]

Since the understanding that apostles are present in the workplace is new, obviously much more needs to be done in helping to identify them.

One who has moved strongly in this direction is Rich Marshall, author of the foundational work *God@Work*. Marshall has now released *God@Work, Volume 2,* in which he lists characteristics of marketplace apostles. He uses the term "marketplace apostles" sparingly; mostly he uses "marketplace ministers" so as not to alienate readers who may not as yet accept the idea of present-day apostles. Marshall's signs of workplace apostles are as follows:

- They perform signs and wonders
- They exhibit authority
- They break bondages
- They transfer wealth
- They hear the voice of God
- They function as biblical entrepreneurs
- They reach nations[5]

The role of apostles in the workplace is so important that I believe they provide the key to two enormously significant gates that must be opened if we are to see the kingdom of God manifested as it should be. Neither one will be opened apart from the active involvement of workplace apostles. One is the gate of social transformation, and the other is the gate of the great transference of wealth. These are the subjects of the next two chapters.

Chapter 3

Let's Take
Dominion Now!

Social transformation, as I have been saying, is one of the strongest words that the Holy Spirit is clearly speaking to the churches today. But before many of us would be prepared to accept that statement at face value, we would need to be assured that what we think we might be hearing from the Holy Spirit is truly biblical. We are sure, for example, that saving souls is biblical, but how about transforming society?

I know this is a crucial question, because for years I would have said that working toward social change should not be considered a part of our Christian duty. I was taught that the world was supposed to get worse and worse, and the more it did, the closer Christ's second coming would be. I believed that at some low point in history, all true believers would be snatched out of the earth and that those left behind would go through seven of the worst years of all, just prior to the Lord's glorious appearing. Meanwhile, our job was to spread the gospel and get as many souls saved as possible so that they would be taken up with us in the rapture whenever it might come, and the sooner the better. However, I am now certain that there is a more accurate and a more biblical way of understanding God's mission for us, which I'll try to explain as convincingly as I can in this chapter.

Having said that, my hope is that not too many readers who happen to love the famous *Left Behind* series of books will decide to shut the book at this point and go no further. I will go on record as saying that I personally have read *every* one of the *Left Behind* series, and if more books come out, I plan on reading them as well. I have enjoyed each of them greatly, keeping in mind that they are fiction, pure and simple.

Back to the Beginning

An excellent starting point to explain the mission God gave us is to go to the story of creation itself. We are told in Genesis 1 that God created the earth and everything in it in five days, and then on the sixth day He created Adam and Eve. He created them, male and female, in His image. When He did, He blessed them and said, "Be fruitful and multiply; fill the earth and subdue it; have dominion over the fish of the sea, over the birds of the air, and over every living thing that moves on the earth" (Gen. 1:28).

You may notice that I included that word "dominion" in the title of this chapter: "Let's Take Dominion Now!" Why? Because the first words God spoke to humans, as recorded in the Bible, includes the mandate to "have dominion." It wasn't just Adam and Eve who were to have dominion; it was the whole human race that would "fill the earth" after Adam and Eve began being fruitful and multiplying. Apparently, having dominion over the rest of creation is something built into God's original design for us humans; it is not an afterthought. To the extent that humans fail to have dominion, they also fail to live up to the fullness of their divine destiny.

"Your Kingdom Come"

Moving from the Old Testament to the New Testament, let's look at the Lord's Prayer, an excellent starting point for understanding our mission in the world. When Jesus' disciples asked Him to teach them to pray, He replied, "In this manner, therefore pray: Our Father in heaven, hallowed be Your name. Your kingdom come. Your will be done on earth as it is in heaven" (Matt. 6:9-10).

God's ideal for human society is obviously the society that He directly oversees in heaven. It would follow, therefore, that this should also be the way that we live here on Earth, and that is what we should be praying for. Heaven is a place of peace and prosperity and health and happiness and morality and selflessness and well-being and harmony and understanding and kindness and high worship. To the extent that the society in which we live is not characterized by such qualities of life, it falls short of what God wants it to be. Since we are God's people, we are responsible to do whatever we can to help our communities meet God's expectations. I like the way that Bill Hamon expresses this idea: "The Lord has called us to be cultural architects—not just cultural critics."[1]

As you can see, all of this can be summarized in the expression that we are using more than ever these days, namely, *social transformation.*

A Long Road

I'm sad to say that it took us evangelical Christians a considerable amount of time to get to where we are today. It was too long a road. But the good news is that we are finally arriving.

To trace this back, the beginning centuries of Christianity were a time of severe persecution. For the most part, believers did not have the power to transform the society of the Roman Empire, where most of them found themselves. Things changed for them in the fourth century, when the Roman emperor Constantine professed conversion to Christianity, stopped the persecution and declared his Roman Empire "Christian." However, this new unholy fusion of church and state soon became corrupt, and both the church and society went downhill during the Middle Ages. Unfortunately, God's will was not being done on Earth as it was in heaven!

Then the Protestant Reformation came along in the sixteenth century, led by Martin Luther and John Calvin. Luther's views of Scripture and of justification by faith produced one of the most positive changes in church history. However, he had a dualistic view of the church against the world, and therefore he was never much inclined to push the church toward the mission of transforming society. Calvin, on the other hand, taught that believers are responsible for social transformation, and his followers began to believe that we have a cultural mandate (the mandate to transform society) as well as an evangelistic one (the mandate to save souls). One famous Calvinist, pastor and theologian Abraham Kuyper (1837-1920), lived this out, entered politics, became prime minister of the Netherlands and caused tremendous positive changes in society as a result.

Meanwhile, the modern missionary movement began around 1800, after William Carey went to India. While humanitarianism, such as starting schools and hospitals and orphanages, was a standard part of missionary ministry, overt efforts to transform the structures of society itself were few and far between. The evangelical missionary movement featured the evangelistic mandate, but not so much the cultural mandate.

Toward the end of the 1800s, a liberal element of the church began promoting what was called the social gospel. They ended up going to the extreme of advocating that transforming society was all that was necessary and that saving souls was an idea of the past. Naturally, Bible-believing evangelicals reacted strongly against this, and they went to the opposite extreme of rejecting social ministry altogether. Taking dominion? That was, to them, something for liberals who didn't believe the Bible!

That history brings us up to the times that some of us living today can remember personally. I am among them. As an evangelical missionary in Bolivia during the 1950s and 1960s, I was of the persuasion that our task was to save souls, make disciples and multiply churches. Period.

The Congress in Lausanne

A significant change came in 1974 when the evangelical movement, led by Billy Graham, held the International Congress on World Evangelization in Lausanne, Switzerland. At that point, evangelicals began reconsidering the place of the cultural mandate alongside the evangelistic mandate within the total mission of the church. This was a very important shift for those of us who now advocate social transformation. It turned out to be only a partial shift, however, in that the Lausanne Covenant insisted on subordinating the cultural mandate to the evangelistic mandate. Still, we evangelicals then began to have social responsibility on our radar screens, even though it wasn't front and center.

One event that did help to move social issues to the front and center of our agenda, particularly among evangelicals who were tuned in to the charismatic movement, was the publication in 1990 of John Dawson's best-selling book *Taking Our Cities for God*. The concept of taking a city was a tremendous innovation.

After Dawson wrote his book, the literature expanded rapidly. He was joined by authors such as Ed Silvoso, George Otis, Jr., Ted Haggard, Jack Hayford, Frank Damazio, Alistair Petrie and others. The movement is concisely summarized in Jack Dennison's *City Reaching*. Those who were involved experimented with a variety of terms such as "taking cities," "reaching cities," "prayer evangelism," "reaching a nation," "reformation," "community transformation," "revival" and "reconstruction." By 2000, however, the most generally accepted term became "social transformation." In 2005, Luis Bush gave form to the movement by helping to organize a series of events called Transform World, with the first international meeting held in Indonesia.

Time for Action!

Now that we have social transformation on our evangelical agendas, it is time for action. I regard "social transformation" as the *concept* term. However, the *action* term that will best set us on the road toward that goal is "taking dominion."

Regrettably, a number of church leaders today have developed a negative reaction to the term "Dominion Theology." The root of this goes back to that period of time following World War II that I discussed in the last chapter, when several pioneering movements attempted to resurrect the offices of apostle and prophet. Some leaders of those movements began to advocate "Dominion Theology," using that very term. A related movement taught what they called Kingdom Now Theology. Some strong critics of these movements did their best to discredit their innovative leaders, and part of their procedure became an attack on Dominion Theology and Kingdom Now Theology. The critics were certainly right in pointing out a number of the errors of these pioneers both in theory and in practice, but in my opinion some of the critics opened doors for their own set of damaging extremes. Rejecting Dominion Theology and Kingdom Now Theology was one of them.

Let me illustrate this with a recent experience of my own. One Sunday I was teaching a congregation the basics of what I have been advocating in this book. As I spoke that day, I did not mention the word "dominion."

When I finished, I spent time interacting with members of the congregation who wished to talk to me. One of them, after greeting me, said words to this effect: "Peter, isn't there a danger that what you were talking about could be interpreted as Dominion Theology?" The unspoken implication was a warning that I might be in danger of crossing the boundary line into what had become to many a standard heresy. I could see the look of surprise on his face when I replied straightforwardly, "What I'm teaching is, in fact, Dominion Theology." He respected me enough to respond that he would have to look into Dominion Theology a bit more carefully from then on.

While we are on the subject, allow me to be more specific about what I brought up at the beginning of this chapter concerning the *Left Behind* series. For most of the twentieth century, the prevailing eschatology (doctrine of the end times) of evangelicals was premillenialism. We expected the kingdom of God to come after Jesus returned to the earth. Therefore, we were not called to attempt to usher in God's kingdom. God would do that in His own time. Entire denominations have elevated premillenialism to an absolute doctrinal principle alongside doctrines such as the deity of Christ and justification by faith. This explains why some would reject Dominion Theology and Kingdom Now Theology. A paradigm shift toward social transformation would force them to leave their eschatological comfort zone.

The Danger of Transformation Fatigue

The question now arises, How effective have our efforts been since the cultural mandate joined the evangelistic mandate on our agendas?

We have wonderful results to report concerning the implementation of the evangelistic mandate. For example, we began the decade of the 1990s with 1,735 significant unreached people groups, and by 2000 all except fewer than 500 had initial church-planting movements in them. Unprecedented evangelistic harvests are being reaped in global hot spots such as China, Nigeria, Indonesia, India and Brazil. Some nations, like Uganda and Guatemala, are now more than 50 percent born-again evangelical believers.

But how about the cultural mandate? Since 1990, as I have explained, city transformation has been high on our priority lists. That, as I write this, was 15 years ago. Our best top-level Christian leadership has been involved with this in city after city across America. God has been providing incredible new tools for getting the job done—tools such as identificational repentance; spiritual mapping; strategic prophetic prayer; massive all-night, stadium prayer events; strategic-level spiritual warfare; prayer journeys; pastoral unity; and the concept of the church of the city. In addition, Bill Bright, Elmer Towns and others made fasting popular, and I would guess that somewhere around half of American evangelical pastors have now experienced 40-day fasts.

However, we cannot point to a single city in America that has been transformed in all of those 15 years!

I foresee a danger—the danger of transformation fatigue! We must not become weary of well-doing. Satan would love to quench this move of the Holy Spirit by bringing a cloud of despair and hopelessness. Let's bind that wicked spirit of fatigue and move forward with faith, for "without faith it is impossible to please Him" (Heb. 11:6).

Faith-Building Examples

To know that it can be done is a powerful faith builder. A city *can* be transformed. Let's look at two examples of this, one from history and one from today.

Florence, Italy

Let's look back to Florence, Italy, before the Protestant Reformation. Girolamo Savanarola was a reformer before his time. He was a precursor of things to come. He prayed. He prophesied. He preached. He had an apostolic anointing to influence large numbers of people. Here is one account of what happened to his city:

> The wicked city government [of Florence] was overthrown, and Savanarola taught the people to set up a democratic form of

government. The revival brought tremendous moral change. The people stopped reading vile and worldly books. Merchants made restitution to the people for the excessive profits they had been making. Hoodlums and street urchins stopped singing sinful songs and began to sing hymns in the streets. Carnivals were forbidden and forsaken.

Huge bonfires were made of worldly books and obscene pictures, masks, and wigs. A great octagonal pyramid of worldly objects was erected in the public square in Florence. It towered in seven stages sixty feet high and 240 feet in circumference. While bells tolled, the people sang hymns and the fire burned.[2]

In Florence, God's will was being done on Earth as it is in heaven!

Almolonga, Guatemala

Twice I have visited Almolonga, Guatemala, a city of about 20,000 indigenous people, located deep in the Guatemalan highlands. What I saw was a true faith builder for city transformation.

The process began in the mid-1970s when Mariano Riscajche, a struggling pastor, began casting out demons, especially the demon of alcoholism. Since then, transformation has come in several areas:

- *Spiritual awakening.* The percentage of born-again Christians in Almolonga has risen dramatically from less than 5 percent to 90 percent at the present time. Previously the city was under a dark cloud of Satanic oppression, orchestrated by the ruling territorial spirit, Maximón. But now that the forces of evil have been pushed back, Almolonga enjoys open heavens, allowing the blessings of God to be poured out. Large, attractive churches are among the most prominent architectural features of the city's hilly landscape.
- *Social harmony.* Almolonga was filled with dysfunctional families that were devastated by drunkenness, adultery, wife abuse and child neglect; but now the city is filled with happy marriages, clean homes, wholesome schools and friendly people.

- *Material prosperity.* Almolonga no longer suffers poverty caused by chronic drought and famine; now it enjoys agricultural plenty, producing vegetables that are record-breaking in size. Carrots, for example, are the size of a man's forearm. Crops are now sustained by a natural water supply that comes up from the ground rather than being dependent on rainfall. Farmers deliver their produce throughout Central America in Mercedes trucks that they purchase for cash, christening each one with a Christian name.

- *Law and order.* Until Almolonga was transformed, it had no fewer than six crowded jails to deal with robbery, lawlessness and violence in the streets. Several years ago, however, the last jail was closed because of the absence of crime, and it was turned into a Hall of Honor, which is used for weddings and other celebrations.

- *Physical and ecological transformation.* Almolonga was constantly victimized by plagues, diseases and violent storms. These have now disappeared, while the neighboring city of Zunil, only 3 kilometers away, which still honors the idol of Maximón, remains victimized by those very things.

Almolonga is known for enjoying one of the highest qualities of life in all of Central America. Many people travel internationally to Almolonga just to see firsthand what God's hand on city transformation really looks like.

What Is Our Goal?

With Christian leaders on all continents now tuning in to what the Spirit is saying to the churches about social transformation, it is important that, as much as possible, we all get on the same page concerning essential parts of the social-transformation equation. One of these essential parts, obviously, is the goal.

Eddie Long, pastor of the 25,000-strong New Birth Missionary Baptist Church in Atlanta, Georgia, has a passion for social transformation. His goal is clear. It is reflected in the title of his powerful book on the subject: *Taking Over*. Long writes, "Jesus took away Satan's keys and power at Calvary, and it is up to us to come along behind and subdue and have dominion over every evil work and every servant of evil."[3]

The Measure for Success

If we agree that we need to move with God for taking over a certain city, how will we know if and when we have succeeded? I think that a biblically rooted measure for success would be the birth of a new creation: "Therefore, if anyone is in Christ, he is a new creation; old things have passed away; behold, all things have become new" (2 Cor. 5:17). If this is what the Bible expects of individuals who are transformed, why should we expect less of a city? If individuals can be born again, why can't cities, made up of many individuals, be born again?

Watered-Down Transformation

I keep a file of transformation reports—anecdotes that truly are exciting, faith-building and glorifying to God. Here are some examples from different American cities:

- The crime rate has gone down.
- Adult bookstores began to close after prayerwalking.
- Affordable housing is being built in the slums.
- Two psychics moved out of town.
- The rate of unemployment is much lower.
- Employees of banks pray with their customers regularly and play praise music during the day.
- A gay bar went out of business.
- The mayor and the chief of police have been born again.
- The biggest drug bust in the city's history just occurred.
- A Christian Chamber of Commerce was organized.
- The newspapers are giving more favorable coverage to the churches and their activities.
- Abortion clinics have shut down.
- The school system has taken a turn for the better.

Certainly we would applaud every one of these wonderful reports. But none of them alone, nor any combination of all of them, would verify that a city has been transformed (past tense). I believe that these reports are predicated on a watered-down version of transformation.

In the global leadership circles in which I move, the focus of some of my friends is the process of transformation. My thought is that we should not be satisfied with reporting stages of the process as if they were the final goal. No, we should focus on complete transformation. I am not questioning the importance of reporting the process, but I want to emphasize that the process is only a means toward the end, not the end in itself.

True Transformation

What, then, should our goal be? I think it should be *sociologically verifiable transformation.* In other words, an independent professional sociologist, using standard social scientific measuring instruments, would draw the conclusion that the city has been transformed. One reason that I use Almolonga, Guatemala, as an example is that such a thing was done there. The Guatemalan equivalent of *Time* magazine, *Crónica Semanal,* sent its researchers to Almolonga and ran a cover story on the amazing transformation of the city. The title of the cover story was "The Defeat of Maximón!"

Among other things, the article says, "The cult of Maximón and its followers has been reduced to a mere handful of individuals; and due to his downfall, the men of the city no longer drink liquor because of their evangelical faith. Therefore the annual festival to the idol . . . is now financed only by money collected from sightseeing tours of Japanese, Germans and Americans."[4]

By using the term "sociologically verifiable transformation," I am not trying to insist that professional academia be brought into the picture, although it wouldn't be a bad idea. No, the *Crónica Semanal* cover story was done by a competent investigative journalist.

Another convincing example of a grassroots change-agent reporting on substantial progress toward transformation is Eddie Long of Atlanta, whom I quoted previously. Here is Long's report:

Today I can honestly say that metropolitan Atlanta would miss [New Birth Missionary Baptist Church] very much if something caused us to move away or shut down. The New Birth congregation finances and operates vital support programs in the city and pumps large sums of money and thousands of volunteer hours into key areas such as youth offender intervention programs, public school programs, and support and outreach programs for homeless women and children. We are involved in every aspect of life, and we are making a major impact in the Atlanta metropolitan areas.

This, in turn, is causing us to gain major footholds in the city infrastructure, . . . the criminal court system, public high schools, the Georgia State Senate, the United States Senate, and even into the White House itself. . . . When you are a politician in a major metropolitan area, it isn't wise to dismiss or ignore a highly unified, committed, and motivated group of voters exceeding twenty-two thousand people representing almost every voting precinct in your city.[5]

Whether Atlanta will be transformed as completely as Almolonga remains to be seen. However, it would be fair to say that it has made considerable progress toward complying with our strict definition, that of sociologically verifiable transformation. If we can agree to use this definition, we then reaffirm our belief that our city can become a new creation in Christ Jesus, and we can collectively move forward toward that goal.

Our Biblical Mandate

At the beginning of this chapter, I quoted Genesis 1:28, where God explicitly indicates that His original design was for human beings to take dominion over all of creation. However, Adam and Eve, tempted by Satan, proceeded to turn history upside down. By disobeying God and breaking his relationship with the Creator, Adam lost his integrity, his rulership and his personal destiny. He became a sinner and was no longer in the pure image of God. And worse yet, he passed his fallen nature down genetically through every human generation since.

Meanwhile, Satan was accomplishing his own purpose in the Garden of Eden. To understand this in depth, think of the difference between power and authority. If, for example, I own a .338 Winchester Magnum rifle, I have power. However, I cannot discharge that rifle in the city of Colorado Springs because I do not have the authority to do so. On the other hand, if I happened to be a Colorado Springs police officer with the same rifle, I would then have not only the power but also the authority to use that power.

When Lucifer was in heaven, he had both power and authority. However, when Satan was cast from heaven, he retained his power, but he lost his authority. Adam was given authority to take dominion over creation, but he fell and created a vacuum of authority over God's creation. Satan then stepped in, usurped Adam's authority and became "the god of this age" (2 Cor. 4:4) and "the prince of the power of the air" (Eph. 2:2) and "the ruler of this world" (John 14:30). John went so far as to affirm that "the whole world lies under the sway of the wicked one" (1 John 5:19).

How much authority, or dominion, did Satan actually acquire? Let's go to Jesus' third temptation to find out. Presuming that the temptations were real and not just someone's dream or a figment of someone's imagination, we see Satan literally taking Jesus up on a high mountain. Satan then shows Jesus all (not just a few!) of the kingdoms of the world. Then Satan says, "All these [kingdoms] I will give You if You will fall down and worship me" (Matt. 4:9). My point is that this temptation could only have been real if Satan actually had the power and the authority to deliver the kingdoms to Jesus. Significantly enough, Jesus never once questioned the validity of Satan's claim over the kingdoms of the world.

Jesus, the Second Adam

Although Jesus never questioned Satan's dominion, He came to earth expressly to take it away from him. Jesus came as the second, or last, Adam (see 1 Cor. 15:45-47). The first Adam lost dominion; the second Adam will regain it. This was a new beginning of history. It is part of the New

Covenant, not the Old Covenant. Jesus brought a new kingdom, namely, the kingdom of God.

The first to announce the Kingdom was John the Baptist. He preached in the wilderness and said, "Repent, for the kingdom of [God] is at hand" (Matt. 3:2). This was the D-day of the invasion of the kingdom of Satan. During World War II, when the Allies established a beachhead in France on D-day, everyone knew that the war in the European theater was over. However, many more battles still needed to be fought until Hitler was finally defeated. Similarly, Jesus' coming as the second Adam marked the beginning of the end of Satan's defeat. It is now up to us, empowered by the Holy Spirit, to fight the battles needed to finish it.

Jesus preached the gospel of the Kingdom; the apostles preached the gospel of the Kingdom; and He expects us to preach the gospel of the Kingdom (see Matt. 24:14). What is the gospel of the Kingdom?

After the temptation, Jesus went to the synagogue in His hometown of Nazareth and announced His agenda. We can surmise that this would be the basic content of the gospel of the Kingdom. It included preaching good news to the poor, healing the brokenhearted, bringing deliverance to the captives, giving sight to the blind, freeing the oppressed and preaching the acceptable year of the Lord (see Luke 4:18-19).

A Fresh View of Scripture

Following this pattern, our new paradigm for taking dominion includes a dual task: the evangelistic mandate (saving souls) and the cultural mandate (transforming society). Once we have this in mind, we will have mental tools to take a fresh look at two biblical passages that have been favorites of us evangelicals.

The first is Luke 19:10, which reads, "For the Son of Man has come to seek and to save that which was lost." Our old paradigm interpretation would make it read, "to save those who were lost." But it does not say this. It says "*that* which was lost." What is "that"? It is dominion over creation, which was lost in the Garden of Eden by the first Adam. Jesus, as the second Adam, wants to mobilize us to take back what the enemy has stolen.

The second passage is the Great Commission, found in Matthew 28:19-20. Jesus says, "Go therefore and make disciples of all the nations." It does not tell us to make disciples of *individuals* in all the nations, which has been our standard, old-paradigm interpretation. Instead, we are supposed to make disciples of *panta ta ethne,* which in Greek means all ethnic units or social units or people groups. This is a term that denotes sociological groupings of individuals. The whole unit, or nation (including, of course, the individuals who belong to it), is supposed to be Jesus' collective disciple and to observe in that society what Jesus commanded. We now see that the Great Commission's biblical goal is nothing short of social transformation.

Love L.A.

I have used the bulk of this chapter to explain the ins and outs of the new paradigm that we have for social transformation, namely, taking dominion. Now I want to show how the church in the workplace is absolutely essential for the practical outworking of this process.

As I have mentioned, since 1990, we Christian leaders in America have been working on taking dominion, specifically city transformation. I lamented the fact that even with involving the best of our church leadership and employing the incredible new spiritual tools that God revealed to us, we have ended up with meager results.

For example, I lived in the Los Angeles area for most of the 1990s, when I also happened to be one of the leaders of the global prayer movement. Cities all over America were enthusiastically organizing united prayer movements on a scale never before seen in our nation. One of the most notable movements of united prayer during that decade emerged in Los Angeles. Called "Love L.A.," it was headed up by two of our highest-profile national Christian leaders, Lloyd Ogilvie and Jack Hayford. Ogilvie, pastor of Hollywood Presbyterian Church, attracted leaders of traditional denominations. Hayford, pastor of the Foursquare Church On The Way, attracted Pentecostals, charismatics and evangelicals.

The meetings were held once a month in Hollywood Presbyterian Church, hosted by Ogilvie. Only those recognized as leaders could come. Hayford served as the MC. Never before in history had the leaders from churches and ministries in the Los Angeles Basin gathered together on a regular basis in both quantity and quality as they did in Love L.A. The meetings were characterized by exalting worship, powerful prayer, identificational repentance, ethnic reconciliation, humility and brokenness, a burden for the poor and oppressed, cries to God for mercy, pleas for a new Pentecost, openness to fresh revelation, confession of sin, healing, genuine sorrow for injustices in the city, prayer for those in authority, and passion for the lost.

We met not just once, but month after month, year after year. Few cities in the United States surpassed Love L.A. in fervency, intensity, breadth and spiritual power. Love L.A. had a beneficial effect on the city. It was reported that both the crime rate and gang warfare were greatly reduced. A number of porn stores went out of business. Leaders noted a more pervasive sense of morality in the Los Angeles area than previously. The mayor of Los Angeles personally commended Hayford and others for the positive role that the church was playing in the city.

However, let's fast-forward to 2004, several years after Love L.A. ended. Had Los Angeles been transformed by Love L.A.? To answer this, let's look at what Jack Hayford himself wrote in 2004 concerning Los Angeles:

> The simple facts alone, my city's being torn on the inside by gang violence and murder, polluted by homosexuality and pornography on the dark side, and suffocated with pride, self-centered snobbishness and sensuality on the "show" side, is enough to self-destruct us.[6]

Was Love L.A. effective in bringing transformation to Los Angeles? It was a noble effort, characterized by hard work, personal growth, new connections between leaders, a higher level of Christian unity in the city, favorable press coverage, but with all that, not much ongoing social transformation!

What Is Missing?

How do we explain the fact that with the best leadership, with state-of-the-art spiritual methodologies, with commitment of time, money and energy toward city transformation, the results still are not there? I have described Los Angeles because that is the prayer effort in which I was most personally involved, but I have heard similar reports from numerous other cities.

There are at least four ways that this could be explained:

1. *We have the wrong goal.* We have no Christian mandate for city transformation, and therefore we are out of the will of God. It goes without saying that I cannot accept this explanation.

2. *We have the right goal, but we are using the wrong methods.* If this is the case, we have been victims of massive deception, because Christian leadership across the board has regarded our methodology as originating with the Holy Spirit and it has been developed by some of the most gifted and godly servants of the Lord.

3. *We have the right goal and the right methods, but we need to do it more.* In other words, if we have been working toward social transformation in America for 15 years, we need to do the same things for another 15 years and hope for the best. This explanation does not appeal to me because in 15 years, I will be 90 years old!

4. *Our goal and methods are good, but there is something missing.* I like this explanation the best. Let's look into it more. We can still use the same methods that surfaced in the 1990s that we have since fine-tuned, but we need to add something to the equation.

What, then, is missing?

I believe it will help matters a great deal if we can avoid trivial answers to this question. For example, I recently received a rather lengthy report related to winning the war for social transformation. In it, the author suggested that three things were needed in order for us to turn the corner and see results: intimacy with God, unity in the regional church, and holiness and righteousness. I read that with dismay, because for 15 years we have been preaching those three things fervently and have been doing our best to attain them. All were present in Love L.A. I agree that we cannot do without these things, but analytically speaking, I cannot see how any of these would provide a tipping point.

Apostolic Leadership

During the 1990s, we knew very little about apostolic leadership. Neither did we know much about the church in the workplace. But now we do. In chapter 1, I tried to make a case for the church in the workplace, and in chapter 2, I argued that there are apostles in the workplace. We need to move beyond the 1990s and integrate these concepts into our social-transformation efforts.

Let's look, once again, at the social-transformation graphic.

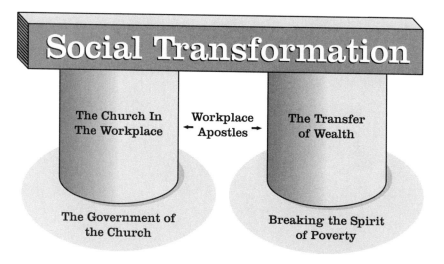

One of the two major columns that support social transformation is the church in the workplace, and workplace apostles help to tie the whole structure together.

A very important role in social transformation is that of territorial apostles. These are apostles to whom God has assigned key apostolic authority over a certain geographical region. I have no doubt that some nuclear-church apostles are also God-ordained territorial apostles. However, this new paradigm of the church in the workplace has brought me to the strong conclusion that the majority of territorial apostles will probably turn out to be *extended-church* apostles rather than *nuclear-church* apostles.

This means that we need to get on with the task of identifying workplace apostles, writing their job descriptions, commissioning them and supporting and encouraging them in every way. Until we do, stories contributing to transformation fatigue are likely to increase. We will continue to wonder why it is so difficult to implement the commission that Jesus, the second Adam, has given us—the commission to take dominion.

Let's decide to move forward. Let's take dominion now!

Chapter 4

From Poverty
to Prosperity

One of the major hypotheses of this book is that the kingdom of God of the twenty-first century will not advance until two things are in place: the activity of the Body of Christ in the workplace and the transfer of wealth. For this to occur, recognized, productive workplace apostles must be functioning in the workplace.

My working diagram of how the different pieces of the new paradigm fit together shows that one of the columns supporting the overall objective of social transformation is the transfer of wealth. Here is the way it looks:

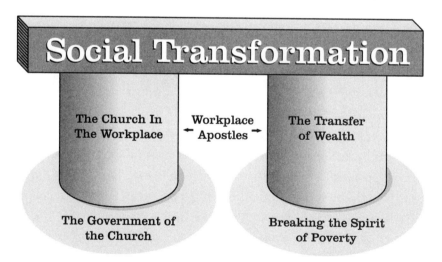

I like the way that Joe Johnson, editor of the magazine *Business Reform*, explains the need for wealth in social transformation. He likens a culture to a highway with many vehicles going in different directions. Some are heading in a godly direction, while others are moving in an ungodly direction. All require fuel. He writes, "According to God's providence, *business controls the supply of fuel.*"[1]

If the vehicles with an ungodly worldview have been well-fueled, while those with a biblical worldview "have been sitting around collecting dust,"[2] we will get nowhere in seeing our society transformed. What needs to be done? Johnson answers, "The church must reach out to the business community, accurately preach the Word of God to business, and help the flock build businesses with a biblical worldview."[3] In my opinion, although Johnson does not go in this direction, seeing that this happens will be a major role of workplace apostles. Joe Johnson goes on to say that when the Christian business community controls the fuel supply, "the problem that is so prominent today of solid Christian organizations not having enough money to make a dent in society will become just a part of history."[4]

Changing History

Speaking of history, please allow me to make a radical statement: When you think of it, there have been three factors throughout all of human history that have changed society far more than anything else, namely, violence, knowledge and wealth. And the greatest of these is wealth. No, I'm not trying to coin a new Bible verse, but I am attempting to emphasize, as strongly as I can, that wealth is the indispensable fuel for our social-transformation vehicles.

Notice in the social-transformation graphic that the base upon which the transfer-of-wealth column stands is labeled "Breaking the spirit of poverty." I believe that in order to break this spirit, we must begin by accurately understanding it. That is why I call this chapter "From Poverty to Prosperity." Once we deal realistically with the evil spirit of poverty that has plagued the church for far too long, we will then begin to open doors to the opposite spirit, namely, the spirit of prosperity.

For some time, God has been telling us through the prophets that He desires to release large amounts of wealth for advancing the kingdom of God. Some knowledgeable individuals, such as Chuck Pierce, trace these prophecies back to around 1992. They may go back even farther. It is important to keep in mind that the prophets to whom I am referring are among the most respected and accurate prophets in the church today. There should be no question that they are accurately communicating words from God.

God's Timing

Since God has said that He desires to release wealth, but we haven't seen widespread release yet, there must be a timing factor involved. While there are some indications at this writing that the release is already beginning, it is still worthwhile to ask what God might be waiting for. I believe that getting workplace apostles in their proper place would be one thing He is waiting for. Barbara Wentroble thinks that another is "getting rid of a poverty mindset." She writes, "Many prophecies are coming forth about the transference of wealth. God wants to position us to receive this wealth for Kingdom purposes. We must deal with any old religious or traditional mindsets that can hinder our faith. Believe the Lord to bring in finances that will help you reach your destiny."[5]

When this release comes, which it will, we will enter a time of abundance. Some will receive it, and some will not. Those who remain bound by the spirit of poverty will lose out. A poverty mind-set is not just a psychological problem. We are dealing with nothing less than a company of high-ranking demons assigned by the enemy to hinder the people of God from stepping up and taking their rightful dominion over God's creation.

The Blessing of Prosperity

Let's understand that it is God's will for His people to prosper, not to be poor. The Bible affirms that those who obey God receive His best. What is God's best? It is laid out in detail in Deuteronomy 28:1-14. Here is just one aspect: "The LORD will grant you abundant prosperity—in the fruit of your womb, the young of your livestock and the crops of your ground—in the land he swore to your forefathers to give you" (Deut. 28:11, *NIV*).

The theme is carried through the ages to what might have been the last book of the Bible to be written, 3 John. "Beloved, I pray that you may prosper in all things and be in health, just as your soul prospers" (3 John 2). This Scripture helps us realize that prosperity is multidimensional, not limited to material things. In my opinion, prosperity has four facets: material prosperity, spiritual prosperity, physical prosperity and social prosperity.

The Curse of Poverty

The opposite of prosperity is poverty. If prosperity is the will of God, then poverty must be the will of the devil. Consequently, a reasonable assumption would be that there is a demonic spirit of poverty active in the world today. This is an agent of Satan assigned to prevent people from prospering by keeping them in a state of poverty.

Poverty is nothing less than a curse. The first part of Deuteronomy 28, as we have seen, promises prosperity to those who obey the Lord. However, the second part of the same chapter, verses 15-68, promises poverty for those who refuse to obey. "All these curses will come upon you," verse 15 reads. One of the curses is this: "You shall serve your enemies, whom the LORD will send against you, in hunger, in thirst, in nakedness, and in need of everything; and He will put a yoke of iron on your neck until He has destroyed you" (Deut. 28:48).

I am aware that as soon as I start affirming prosperity as godly, certain believers will be rubbed the wrong way. Why is this? It is because the spirit of poverty, linked up with the spirit of religion, has been more successful through the years than it should have been. One of its greatest victories has been to promote the doctrine through most of mainstream Christianity that piety is directly proportional to poverty.

Medieval Monasticism

This unbiblical mind-set gained strength around the fourth century, when the church, aligned with Emperor Constantine, began to open the door to a Greek, rather than a biblical Hebrew, worldview. Greek thinking, as we saw in chapter 1, promoted the idea of the spiritual aspect of life as superior to the material aspect of life. The conclusion was that the more spiritual you are, the less material you will be. The monasteries and their monks adopted this philosophy and promoted it throughout the Middle Ages. Before long, all clergy, in order to attest their superior spirituality, were obligated to take vows of poverty, chastity and obedience.

Most believers nowadays have rejected the idea that chastity is necessarily saintly. We agree that sexuality is a gift from God. At the same time, I suspect that we might have gone a bit overboard in reacting against the monastic ideal of obedience. Most of us probably could use a more positive attitude toward submission. And unfortunately, the vow of poverty has persisted in our churches. It has become an institutional curse over the Body of Christ that badly needs to be broken. The yoke of medieval monasticism has been on our shoulders much too long. It is a burden, perhaps even a curse, that we should not be expected to bear.

Having said that, I'd like to emphasize that I believe we are beginning to move in the right direction. It will not be long before many of us agree that we should move from poverty to prosperity. For about 35 years, God has been preparing His people for this new mind-set. As I look back, I see four major steps that the Body of Christ has taken toward rejecting the oppression of the spirit of poverty.

Rejecting the Spirit of Poverty

Step 1: The Word-Faith Movement

The first step was the emergence of the Word-Faith Movement in the early 1970s. Some of the more visible leaders of this movement were Kenneth Hagin, Kenneth Copeland, Frederick K. C. Price and many others. They distinguished themselves by taking literally God's promises for prosperity. They had the faith to hold God to His Word, and as a result, they prospered. They themselves prospered, their ministries prospered, and large numbers of their followers prospered. They prospered materially, spiritually, physically and socially.

Rhema Bible Institute of Tulsa, Oklahoma, became their principal training center. Unlike most other Bible schools and seminaries, Rhema focuses on helping its students gain freedom from the spirit of poverty, along with teaching normal Bible subjects. Rhema students have gone all over the world and have extended the kingdom of God.

Fred Price

For many years, when I lived in the Los Angeles area, Fred Price was my neighbor and my friend. I watched the impressive growth of Crenshaw Christian Center, the church he pastored (and still pastors). I was amazed that the church was able to purchase the Pepperdine University campus in central Los Angeles after Pepperdine moved to another location. I watched the construction of the Faith Dome, containing 10,400 seats, the largest church facility west of the Mississippi. In fact, I was privileged to be one of the speakers at its dedication.

What is so remarkable about Fred Price and Crenshaw Christian Center? This is a church planted in the ghetto of Los Angeles. The converts, mostly African-Americans, were among the poorest of the poor. Welfare, substance abuse, unemployment, violence, dysfunctional families and despair were accepted as a way of life. They were virtual slaves of poverty. However, once these people became involved at Crenshaw Christian Center, they found the faith for a better life. They gained the supernatural power to break the spirit of poverty. They began moving into godly prosperity.

I would not be surprised if statistics showed that Fred Price, even more than any mayor of Los Angeles, has been influential in getting the largest number of African-Americans off the Los Angeles welfare rolls.

Limited Scope

Having said these good things about the Word-Faith Movement, why then didn't the whole Body of Christ pick up on this? Why didn't everybody want to be like Kenneth Hagin or Fred Price? I think there are three reasons.

First, Word-Faith was a charismatic movement. Those who were involved worshiped with exuberance, raised their hands in church services, spoke in tongues, received words from God and healed the sick. Large segments of the Body of Christ, on the other hand, were convinced cessationists, and they could not accept such things in their churches. Anything charismatic, including breaking the spirit of poverty, was seen as an aberrant form of Christianity, something to be avoided. In fact, for most of the mainline denominations in the United States, the Word-Faith Movement was not even on their radar screens.

Second, many believers who were open to charismatic things were not prepared to approve of some of the outward signs of prosperity that many Word-Faith leaders exhibited. They reacted against what seemed to be extremes of personal opulence. Fred Price, for example, chose to drive a Rolls Royce. This was seen by some as a sub-Christian decision, despite the facts that the church had given him the car and that the church members who contributed were delighted to see him drive it.

Third, many church leaders had been captivated by the pervasive force of the spirit of poverty. They were convinced, as were the medieval monks, that poverty reflects piety. Their simple conclusion was that people who live in large homes or have airplanes or drive Rolls Royces could not be very pious.

Fortunately, the pendulum is swinging back. The second-generation Word-Faith leaders are in place, and they are avoiding some of the extravagances. The dividing lines between Word-Faith and the wider Body of Christ are not nearly as sharp as they once were. Word-Faith has been a significant step toward breaking the spirit of poverty off of the entire Body of Christ.

Step 2: The Social-Transformation Movement

The social-transformation movement is a second significant step toward dealing a blow to the spirit of poverty. It became a frequent topic of discussion in the early 1990s and has continued to be so through today. Since the previous chapter was about the social-transformation movement, I need not elaborate in much detail here. Nevertheless, I feel I should emphasize that we must have a more complete understanding of the kingdom of God and of our mandate to take dominion of God's creation if we are to fulfill God's desire that His will be done on Earth as it is in heaven.

I want to reiterate the importance of Jesus' ministry in His hometown of Nazareth after His baptism and temptation. There Jesus gave His first public address in a synagogue, according to Scripture. Consequently, it is not beyond reason to assume that Jesus was setting the agenda for His earthly ministry at that time. He began, "The Spirit of the Lord is upon Me, because He has anointed Me to preach the gospel to the poor" (Luke 4:18). The word "gospel" means good news. Imagine that you are poor, really poor. Your annual income is well below the poverty level. What would be good news for you? The best news possible would be that you are no longer going to be poor. This was the very first thing on Jesus' agenda.

The social-transformation movement believes that the values and lifestyle of the kingdom of God should permeate our communities, our cities, our ethnic groups and our nations. "Your will be done on earth as it is in heaven," Matthew 6:10 reads. I can assure you that in heaven there are no ghettos or welfare rolls or food stamps or rat-infested housing or malnutrition or violence on the streets. The spirit of poverty has no place there, nor should it have a place in our society today.

Step 3: The Church-in-the-Workplace Movement

I explained the concept of the church in the workplace in some detail in chapter 1. Here I want to show how this is a third step toward breaking the spirit of poverty that has plagued our churches. I'm listing it as the third step because, while the movement can be traced back to the 1950s, it really began to escalate in the late 1990s.

The idea behind this is that the people of God are the church (the ekklesia). They are the church on Sundays, but they also remain the church the other six days of the week in the workplace. The terminology I suggest is "nuclear church" for the congregations that meet on Sundays and "extended church" for the people of God in the workplace.

The Church-Workplace Gap

We need to understand this concept as clearly as possible because, unfortunately, there has been a huge gap between the two forms of the same church. Laura Nash, professor of business ethics at Harvard Business School, and Scotty McLennan, dean of Religious Life at Stanford University, did a remarkable sociological study that unearthed this gap. They reported their discoveries in their book *Church on Sunday,*

Work on Monday, which references what I call the nuclear church and the extended church.

Nash and McLennan's findings highlight the grip that the spirit of poverty has attained on our churches. They report that "businesspeople and clergy live in two worlds. Between the two groups lie minefields seeded with attitudes about money, poverty, and the spirit of business—attitudes that can be summarized as those of the yea-sayers and naysayers of capitalism."[6]

They go on to write:

> The clergy tended to represent business as an aggregate concept, centered on money or profit—code words for excessive wealth and exploitation. They saw businesspeople as greedy and selfish; they repeatedly mentioned money as business's primary concern (excessive salaries, consumption lifestyles, materialistic ambitions, the wage gap). Accumulation of wealth had especially negative associations of idolatry, sin, materialism, false values, wrong priorities, selfishness, and most of all injustice against the poor.[7]

The idea that poverty is piety apparently persists.

John Osteen

That poverty equals piety plays out in the common idea that it is normal for preachers to be poor. I love the way that Joel Osteen, author of the best-seller *Your Best Life Now,* tells how this worked in the life of his father, John Osteen. "Daddy grew up with a 'poverty mentality,'" writes Joel.

> That's all he had ever known. When he first started pastoring, the church could pay him only $115 a week. Daddy and Mother could hardly survive on that little amount of money, especially once my siblings and I came along. The most dangerous aspect of their life, however, was that Daddy had come to expect poverty. For a number of years he wasn't even able to accept a blessing when it came.[8]

Joel goes on to tell the story of how his parents once stretched their family budget by hosting the church's guest speaker for a week. After the speaker left, a businessman in the church said that he wanted to cover those extra expenses and more besides, and he handed John Osteen a personal check for a thousand dollars (the equivalent of maybe ten thousand dollars today). Osteen accepted the check, but he insisted on putting it in the church offering.

Joel's comments: "Daddy later admitted that deep down inside, he really preferred to keep the money. He knew that he and Mother needed that money, but he had a false sense of humility. He couldn't receive the blessing. He thought he was doing God a favor by staying poor."[9]

Because of the church-in-the-workplace movement, this gap is closing. More and more people are becoming comfortable with the idea that God calls many of His people to a *ministry* (I have chosen that word carefully) of making money. The spirit of poverty hates this!

Step 4: The Transfer-of-Wealth Movement

The latest of these four steps away from the spirit of poverty is the transfer-of-wealth movement. This is one of the pillars that directly support social transformation, as the diagram at the beginning of this chapter shows. As I have said, prophecies about the transfer of wealth go back to the early 1990s, but the phenomenon itself belongs to the twenty-first century. In my estimation, part of the reason why these huge funds have not previously been released is that God is awaiting clearer recognition of workplace apostles. Workplace apostles have long since been liberated from the spirit of poverty.

When the wealth is released, it will come to God's people through supernatural transfer or the power to get wealth or a combination of the two.

Supernatural Transfer

God at times chooses to transfer wealth to His people supernaturally. The wealth is not produced by the works of the hands of those who receive it. A biblical example of supernatural transfer is the story of the Israelites leaving Egypt, where they had been slaves for 400 years. By the time they crossed the Red Sea and began to move into the desert, they were rich; but they did not earn their wealth by making bricks without straw, the work that they were forced to do. God determined that the wealth of the Egyptians would be transferred to them supernaturally before they left Egypt. That is one reason why Pharaoh tried, unsuccessfully, to recapture them as they were leaving.

The Salvation Army is a recent beneficiary of the largest charitable donation in the history of our country. In 2004, Joan Kroc, the widow of Ray Kroc, founder of McDonald's Corporation, died, leaving the Salvation Army $1.5 billion. The Salvation Army did not gain this money by ringing bells in shopping malls around Christmas time or by coming up with another creative fund-raiser. The Salvation Army received it through supernatural transfer.

The Power to Get Wealth

God also transfers wealth by giving His people the power to get wealth. This is set forth in Deuteronomy 8:18: "And you shall remember the Lord your God, for it is He who gives you power to get wealth, that He may establish His covenant which He swore to your fathers."

An example of this recently occurred in Indonesia with my friend Apostle Alex Tanuseputra. Alex, pastor of a church of 80,000 and leader of an apostolic network of 800 churches, knows nothing of the spirit of poverty. He has not been influenced by medieval monasticism. He is now engaged in the construction of the Jakarta Prayer Tower, which is designed to be the highest building in the world and which will cost some $250 million. The tower's foundation is complete; it cost $25 million, all of which came from Alex's churches in Indonesia.

One of the church members is a coal miner. For five years this man had owned a coal mine that was assessed by satellite as containing 300 million tons of coal. Through those five years he had not been able to mine his coal because the world market was only $20 per ton, so it would not have been profitable. The man told Pastor Alex that he wanted to help with the prayer tower, so Alex started praying for him. When he did, things began to change. China suddenly decided to shut down a large number of its existing coal mines and the ensuing shortage brought the market to $40 per ton. The South Korean government got in touch with him because they needed the coal for electrical production, so he had a buyer. When the coal miner started mining his coal, he had it reassessed and found that instead of containing 300 million tons, the mine contained 1 billion tons! Not only that, but soon after they began to work, they discovered oil!

After the coal miner told me the story of how the Lord gave him power to get wealth, he said, "Peter, my first tithe check for the Jakarta Prayer Tower should be around $45 million!"

A Combination

A third way of activating this transfer is a combination of supernatural action plus the power of God on the person of the recipient. This may well be the most common. Even the Israelites who left Egypt had to take action in order to make it happen. They didn't produce the wealth that God had prepared for them, but they wouldn't have received it if they hadn't taken what God supernaturally provided. The Lord said:

> Every woman shall ask of her neighbor, namely, of her who dwells near her house, articles of silver, articles of gold, and clothing; and you shall put them on your sons and on your daughters. So you shall plunder the Egyptians (Exod. 3:22).

The Bible says that if we do the right things with money, including giving to the poor, to widows and to orphans, "God [will] bless you in all the work of your hand which you do" (Deut. 14:29). In other words, as you go about your daily work, a supernatural dimension will enter the picture to make what you are doing more profitable than ever before.

For example, Richard Fleming, author of *The Glory Returns to the Workplace*, had a fleet of cars in England that he planned to sell and then lease back, hoping to make a profit on the transaction. His company had sent out four proposals and had received three responses, each promising around $145,000 in profit. Then one day God spoke to him and said, "Let Me show you how I can make a profit for you. Go into work as usual, but all you are to do is read your Bible."[10]

It took some faith and not a little explanation to his staff, but Richard obeyed and somehow sustained this unusual behavior for a week. At the end of a week of doing nothing but reading the Bible, Richard received the fourth proposal; and the proposal promised not $145,000 in profit but $325,000! All other conditions were equal to those of the other proposals. Richard and his financial director took two weeks to accept the contract because they were sure that something must have been wrong. Richard writes, "In the end we had to come to the conclusion that God had worked a miracle. The company had 250 staff and made annual profits of $900,000. In one week, God produced one-fifth of our annual profit in response to me being obedient to what He had said."[11]

Jesus, Our Example

To convince Christians to believe the lie that piety equals poverty, the spirit of poverty would have to convince us that Jesus, our role model, was poor. Amazingly, this demon has had tremendous success in doing that. We usually think of His being born in a manger or at one point saying that He had no place to lay His head as evidence. Larry Hutch sums up this false mind-set: "We have religiously and traditionally taught that Jesus was poor, so Christians should be poor."[12]

Hutch goes on to point out that Mary and Joseph first went to the inn to get a room. That means they must have had money to pay for the room.

Regarding the wise men and the gifts they brought to Jesus, Hutch writes, "Gold was not the only priceless gift they offered Christ. Frankincense and myrrh are also precious substances. Furthermore, according to Matthew 2:1, there could have been many wise men. These gifts could have ensured that Jesus and His family lived in comfort."[13] Why shouldn't we see that as a supernatural transference of wealth?

Consider the fact that Joseph later took his family on an unexpected two-year trip to Egypt. That certainly required substantial costs for which he had not previously budgeted. And when Jesus was ministering later on, He had a treasury that financed His ministry team.

No, the idea that Jesus was poor is a myth. He was prosperous and yet He was pious! This is not good news to the spirit of poverty.

The rest of the Bible affirms the same thing, as Chuck Pierce and Robert Heidler point out:

> The Bible teaches in no uncertain terms that poverty is a curse, and the Father does not want His children walking under a curse.
>
> There is a lot of crazy thinking in the Church about this! Let me make this clear. Poverty does not make us holy. Most of the holy men in the Bible were not poor. Abraham was rich. Apart from one brief period of adversity, Job lived his life in incredible abundance. David was a king who enjoyed tremendous wealth. Paul had tremendous success as a church planter. He started many churches and saw many of them grow to thousands of members. All along he boasted that he had all the supplies he needed.[14]

The Potholes Along the Way

If we decide to take the trip from a poverty mind-set to a prosperity mind-set (I assure you that it would be a good decision), we need to be aware that the road from here to there has its share of deep potholes. Let's not jump out of the frying pan of poverty into the fire. What could be the fire? Being ensnared by Mammon!

Some people mistakenly think that Mammon refers to wealth or money. Unfortunately, some versions of the Bible reinforce this thinking by translating the Greek *Mammonas* as "money." Notice that I am writing "Mammon" with a capital *M*. That is because Mammon is the proper name of an evil spirit, just like Wormwood or Leviathan or Baal or Beelzebub are. Jesus said that we cannot serve two masters. "You cannot serve God and [M]ammon" (Matt. 6:24).

Mammon has at least four other spirits working with it to produce potholes on the road toward godly prosperity:

1. *The spirit of greed.* Greed is an excessive desire for material possessions. The spirit of greed causes people to imagine that

their personal well-being relates directly to how much they possess. The Bible says that "the love of money is a root of all kinds of evil, for which some have strayed from the faith in their *greediness*" (1 Tim. 6:10, emphasis added). In Luke 12:16-20, Jesus tells the story of the rich man who kept building bigger and bigger barns to store all his goods. He was rich, so obviously he didn't need more, but the spirit of greed drove him to build them. He never had enough. What did he turn out to be? God called him a fool!

2. *The spirit of covetousness.* While greed focuses on amassing inordinate quantities of wealth, covetousness focuses on desiring specific things that you are not supposed to have, such as your neighbor's house or your neighbor's wife or your neighbor's ox, as we see in the Ten Commandments (see Exod. 20:17). Covetousness is so bad that it is equated with idolatry (see Col. 3:5). The link between idolatry and poverty can be seen in Zechariah's prophecy to the people of Judah, who were worshiping idols. Zechariah declared, "Thus says God: 'Why do you transgress the commandments of the Lord so that you *cannot prosper?*'" (2 Chron. 24:20, emphasis added).

   A modern tool of the spirit of covetousness is the credit card. Credit cards can lead to long-term bondage to debt if they are not paid in full each month. They can open the door to impulse buying. Paying just the minimum monthly payment can result in slavery to poverty. With 18-percent interest rates or more, Mammon definitely has its hand in the credit-card business.

3. *The spirit of parsimony.* Parsimony is stinginess. It can cause rich people to be misers and to live in poverty even though they have wealth. It can prevent people from tithing and giving generous offerings. It captivates people to think that they can't afford something that they need or want when they really can afford it. Those who are enslaved by a spirit of parsimony often drag others, including their family members, with them into that strange form of poverty.

Even among people of moderate income, the spirit of parsimony can cause the bad habit of hoarding. This is especially strong among those who lived through the Great Depression and who experienced the rationing of World War II. The spirit of poverty creates the mentality in people that they may never have enough. A good way to break this is to clean unnecessary accumulations from your house, your garage, your attic and your basement. Push the old out so that the new can flow in.

Nothing I have said here should be seen as contrary to good common sense. The opposite of parsimony is wastefulness, an all-too-common trait among many who have been born into relative affluence. Recycling useful materials rather then contributing them to a landfill will defy the spirit of poverty as well. Thriftiness honors God. We can be good stewards of our resources without falling into stinginess.

4. *The spirit of self-reliance.* Another pothole on the road to prosperity is to think that now that we have wealth, we really don't need God. Wealth grants power, and we begin to think that we are so powerful that we can do anything we want to by ourselves. There is a strong biblical counsel against this in Deuteronomy 8. Just before Moses declares that God is the One who gives us the power to get wealth (see v. 18), he warns of this possibility: "Then you say in your heart, '*My* power and the might of *my* hand have gained *me* this wealth'" (v. 17, emphasis added). Mammon can cause you to pray less and to trust God less. Verse 19 then goes on to sternly warn that such people will perish. Self-reliance is pride, and pride goes before a fall (see Prov. 16:18).

How to Move from Poverty to Prosperity

If you can avoid the potholes and the snare of Mammon, you can safely move toward prosperity. The principles that follow will help you avoid them.

Operate in the Opposite Spirit

The principle of operating in the opposite spirit was popularized in the early 1990s by John Dawson, who is currently the president of Youth With A Mission (YWAM). Dawson explains, "When we have discerned the activity of a principality with a particular characteristic, we need to cultivate the opposite characteristic, not only through resisting temptation but by demonstrating positive action."[15]

The example he gives relates to ministry in Cordoba, Argentina, which has a widespread reputation of being a proud, intellectual city. Dawson writes, "We were discerning a principality attempting to rule the city in the pride of life, so we had to confront it in an opposite spirit with a strategy of personal humility."[16] The positive action that they took was to have 200 YWAMers kneel down on Cordoba's streets and sidewalks with their heads touching the ground. Dawson reports that, as a result, people who were resistant to the gospel turned receptive, and a harvest of souls began!

To apply this principle, suppose we discern a principality that we identify as the spirit of poverty. What is the opposite spirit? Prosperity! So we need to take positive action, as Dawson says. We need to cultivate physical prosperity by taking vitamins, eating a healthy diet, taking nutritional supplements, having annual physical exams, exercising and losing excess weight. We need to cultivate spiritual prosperity by praying, reading God's Word, going to church, receiving deliverance and staying filled with the Holy Spirit. We need to cultivate material prosperity by learning how to receive and enjoy money and material things and how to multiply our wealth.

If we are moving in the opposite spirit, we will be grateful for sufficiency, but we will go beyond that and expect abundance. Sufficiency is having enough only for yourself. However, if you are prosperous, you can rise above simply meeting your own needs and also begin to serve others, helping them to be prosperous as well.

Listen to the Prophets

The Bible says, "Believe in the LORD your God, and you shall be established; believe His prophets, and you shall prosper" (2 Chron. 20:20). I am appalled at the number of Christian leaders in America who firmly believe in the Lord and therefore are well-established, but who, for one reason or another, refuse to recognize the office of prophet or to believe the prophets. According to this Scripture in 2 Chronicles, they are preventing themselves from moving into the full prosperity that God desires for them.

I lived many years (in fact, most of my years in ministry) under the spirit of poverty. I am ashamed to admit that I even taught that God promises only sufficiency, not prosperity! It took a prophet to break the spirit of poverty off of me.

Bill Hamon of Christian International is one of the most recognized and respected prophets today. In 1996, soon after I met him, we were together in a symposium in California. He accurately discerned that, partly because I had lived in austerity for 16 years as a missionary in Bolivia, I had remained in the grip of the spirit of poverty. He didn't know it, but I even had been buying a good bit of my clothing in the Salvation Army thrift store, although I could have afforded better. Hamon gathered a small group of prophets, took me to a side room and decreed that the spirit of poverty would no longer have an influence on my life. He then pulled some money out of his pocket and told the others to do the same. He handed me $170 in cash and said that it was a prophetic act for me personally. I was not to give it away, nor was I to tithe it; but I was to spend it on myself and my wife. So Doris and I went out to a gala dinner and paid the bill with the same cash we received, and we even had some left over. That was a turning point. I was instantly delivered from that malicious demon!

Nine years later I happened to be leading the closing session of the annual meeting of the International Coalition of Apostles (ICA). It was a time of worship, prayer and prophecy. Bill Hamon asked my permission to do a prophetic act from the platform, and I told him to go ahead. Much to my surprise, he announced that, since I had never taken a salary from ICA, it was time for the 400 members who were present to bless me, their leader, with financial gifts. (This had never been done before.) He brought my wife, Doris, to the front with me and challenged the apostles to come forward and lay money at the feet of their apostolic leader. The result? We left with thousands of unexpected dollars in our pockets.

When our plane landed in Colorado Springs, I said, "Doris, your Camry is 10 years old, and it has over 100,000 miles on it. We're no longer gripped by the spirit of poverty. Let's go to the Toyota dealer before we drive home." We did, and Bill Hamon's prophetic act resulted in over half of the money needed for Doris's new Camry.

Believe the prophets and you will prosper!

Delight in the Law of the Lord

Here is a clear Biblical teaching on the pathway leading to prosperity:

> Blessed is the man who walks not in the counsel of the ungodly, nor stands in the path of sinners, nor sits in the seat of the scornful; but his delight is in the law of the LORD, and in His law he meditates day and night. He shall be like a tree planted by the rivers of water, that brings forth its fruit in its season, whose leaf also shall not wither; and *whatever he does shall prosper* (Psalm 1:1-3, emphasis added).

Recognize that God is our Creator, and simply follow His Operator's Manual. Read the Book and delight in His law. Don't break the rules and the door will be open for prosperity. Just don't think that you can make your own rules of life and expect to prosper.

Follow John Wesley's Advice

One of John Wesley's most quoted axioms is the following: "Earn all you can, save all you can, give all you can."[17] This means you should work for the highest salary possible given your circumstances and calling. When you save, you should invest your money to get the highest rate of interest or the highest return on the stock market or the highest profit on venture capital. Jesus commended the men who doubled their two talents and five talents, but scolded the one who did not invest the one talent for a return. Why should you multiply the money that you earn? So you can give away large enough amounts of money to make a difference in extending the kingdom of God.

Tithing is the minimal amount that you should give, because by tithing, you are simply returning to God the 10 percent that is His. In fact, if you fail to do this, not only won't you be blessed, but you also are actually risking a curse (see Mal. 3:8-10). Your offerings over and above the tithe are what will begin to break the spirit of poverty and bring prosperity. Luke 6:38 instructs, "Give, and it will be given to you: good measure, pressed down, shaken together, and running over will be put into your bosom. For with the same measure that you use, it will be measured back to you." Why not take that literally?

Some people say that you should never give in order to get. That would be good advice if the Bible didn't teach differently. But Luke 6:38 says clearly that what you give will be returned in larger quantity. And why would you want this to happen? Because when it does, you can give more. Nothing will take you from poverty to prosperity faster than incremental extravagant giving.

Freedom from Poverty!

Not long ago, Global Harvest Ministries convened a National School of the Prophets conference in Middletown, Ohio. Pastors J.C. and Lynn Collins of New Vision Outreach, a ministry in another part of the state, felt that the Lord had sovereignly directed them to attend the conference, even though they didn't know how they could handle it financially. Lynn was so convinced that God was going to do great things in their lives at the conference that she went on a 21-day fast before it.

The week before they left, the church was broke. They had written the last check on the church's bank account. They had just lost their home. Their personal finances had barely allowed them to buy gasoline, to register for the conference and to pay their motel bill in advance. And what about food? The motel served a complimentary breakfast, but they weren't sure what other meals they would be able to afford.

The first night of the conference, Cindy Jacobs took an offering to go toward the down payment on a new building that Global Harvest Ministries was purchasing. She said that there were some in the audience who were to give all they had and then watch how God would break the spirit of poverty over their lives. When people started going forward to give money, Lynn said to J.C., "Do you feel what I am feeling?" "I don't think so," he replied. "What is it?" She said, "I think we are the ones who should give everything!" J.C. agreed. They emptied her purse and his pockets and went up front with their money, $112 in all. They returned to the motel that night with nothing.

The next morning, J.C. discovered, tucked away in his clothing, a $10 bill that he didn't know he had. It was the gas money they needed to go the 35 miles from their motel to the church. As they drove, J.C. shared that he had dreamed the night before that Lynn was on the platform addressing the entire conference.

When lunch time came, a stranger walked up, said that she was going home early, and asked if they could use a gift certificate to Gold Star Chili for their lunch. They gratefully accepted it. When they returned from lunch, they picked up a $20 bill that was blowing across the parking lot!

Barbara Yoder was the next speaker. During her message, some people started walking forward on their own, throwing money on the platform. J.C. said to Lynn, "Do you feel what I am feeling?" The next thing they knew, they were throwing their $20 bill on the platform. Unbelievably, before Barbara's message was concluded, two different men, both strangers, walked up to J.C. and each handed him a $20 bill!

Later in the afternoon, Lynn introduced herself to me and told me her story. I asked her if she would give her testimony to the 2,000 people there that night. I called her up just before I was going to take up another offering for Global Harvest, which is our custom. However, while Lynn was talking, the Lord said to me, "Give them money." So when she finished, I said a few words about breaking the spirit of poverty, and I pulled out a $100 bill that I kept in my wallet for emergencies. I said, "We're going to send them back with some money. I'm giving them $100 of my personal money, and I want four others of you to come and do the same right now! Let's bless them with $500!"

Then it happened! The Holy Spirit was working so powerfully against the spirit of poverty that the whole crowd got up and began to run to the platform, throwing money at Lynn's feet. I scrapped the idea of taking a Global Harvest offering that night and, instead, I encouraged them to keep coming. Lynn was crying. We called J.C. to join her on the platform. They couldn't believe what they were seeing. They had given everything, and here it was coming back to them in abundance. Several prophets began to declare that the spirit of poverty was being broken off of everyone who was present!

The next morning, I called J.C. and Lynn up to the platform and was able to present to them an envelope, not with the $500 that I first thought we'd give, but with $12,500! Later on, other people approached them and gave them $1,400 more!

A few weeks later, I received a letter from J.C. and Lynn. They wrote,

Here is the tithe from that unforgettable night when we witnessed the spirit of lack and poverty being broken not only in us, but throughout the whole sanctuary. Since that day, we have been receiving many testimonies from other individuals and churches that are experiencing the same thing. The next Sunday in our own church, even before I shared our testimony, we received the largest offering in our four-year history. Over three Sundays we exceeded the amount of offerings we had received in all of last year!

We are receiving invitations to speak all over the place. We have been on Christian talk radio sharing this testimony. We are setting up a website so that others can share their stories. Everywhere we go, churches are experiencing the same break-through. We have launched 10 days of 24-hour prayer and fasting. Other pastors are joining with us. We are expecting true revival and transformation in our community!

The lesson is simple. How do we go from poverty to prosperity? We obey the Lord ("Go to the National School of the Prophets!"). We step out in faith ("We really don't have enough finances, but we'll go any-way."). We give extravagantly ("Do you feel what I feel?"). We humble ourselves (We weep as strangers keep throwing money at our feet.). We rejoice at God's goodness ("That unforgettable night"), and we keep the true goal in sight ("We are expecting revival and social transformation.").

Chapter 5

Workplace
Ministries Today

Many leaders in the extended church consider the release of the July 9, 2001, issue of *Fortune* magazine a watershed event. It came across as a de facto, cultural stamp of approval on a movement that had started some 70 years previously, had moved through various stages of development and had begun accelerating notably in the late 1990s, but that still lacked an assurance that what they were doing could actually contribute toward transforming our society.

The cover story of that issue was "God and Business," and its subtitle was "The Surprising Quest for Spiritual Renewal in the American Workplace." Even *Fortune* seemed a bit self-conscious with such an unusual issue. In fact, the managing editor at that time, Rik Kirkland, wrote,

> God and business? Did you ever expect to see those two words on the cover of this magazine? Me neither. At FORTUNE our articles of faith are limited to belief in free trade, unfettered competition, and the proposition that capitalism works best when companies stick to creating value for shareholders. Our normal beat: mammon.[1]

Kirkland goes on to observe that the article "shows why [faith in the workplace] is a lot more than just another trend *du jour*."[2]

The author of this remarkable piece, Marc Gunther, is a somewhat religious person, describing himself as a "minimally observant Jew who has rediscovered his faith in recent years."[3] He usually covers media, not spiritual things, in his professional beat. He said that once he got into it, he "was amazed at the number of business people, especially baby-boomers, looking for a higher purpose in their lives, willing to talk about their faith publicly, and trying to integrate it into their work."[4]

Here are a few quotes from the *Fortune* article:

[This is] a diverse, mostly unorganized mass of believers—a counter-culture bubbling up all over corporate America—who want to bridge the traditional divide between spirituality and work. Historically, such folk operated below the radar, on their own or in small workplace groups where they prayed or studied the Bible. But now they are getting organized and going public to agitate for change.[5]

When the Gallup Poll asked Americans in 1999 if they felt a need to experience spiritual growth, 78% said yes, up from 20% in 1994; nearly half said they'd had occasion to talk about their faith in the workplace in the past 24 hours.[6]

People who want to mix God and business are rebels on several fronts. They reject the centuries-old American conviction that spirituality is a private matter. They challenge religious thinkers who disdain business as an inherently impure pursuit. . . . They disagree with business people who say that religion is unavoidably divisive.[7]

The Pioneers

When I said that the faith-and-work movement (often called the faith-at-work movement) had been going for 70 years, my historical starting point was 1930, when Christian Business Men's Committee (CBMC) was first formed. CBMC should be considered as one of the two major pioneers of the faith-and-work movement. The other is Full Gospel Business Men's Fellowship International, which dates back to 1951.

Christian Business Men's Committee

CBMC was birthed from a deep desire on the part of a number of

Christian businessmen in Chicago to share their faith with their non-Christian peers. The Great Depression had sunk businessmen in America into deep despair, and many were seeking a new hope. The format of choice was noon-hour evangelistic meetings, featuring not traditional, nuclear-church leaders, but rather fellow businessmen sharing their testimonies of how Jesus Christ had made a difference in their personal lives.

Ted DeMoss, who for many years served as president of CBMC, tells CBMC's story in his book *The Gospel and the Briefcase*. CBMC expanded nationally and internationally. Its activities "ranged from evangelistic street meetings, city-wide evangelism crusades, evangelistic centers for servicemen, to radio programs, men's fellowship meetings, jail services, conferences, and other endeavors aimed at helping people to find their way to Christ."[8] In 1993, CBMC adopted its current vision statement: "Compelled by Christ's love and empowered by God's Spirit, impacting the world by saturating the Business and Professional Community with the Gospel of Jesus Christ by establishing, equipping, and mobilizing teams where we work and live that yield spiritual reproducers."[9]

To blend more with the current culture, CBMC has retained its acronym but changed its name to Connecting Business and Marketplace to Christ. They continue strongly to reach the workplace through events such as luncheons and small-group Bible studies.

Full Gospel Business Men's Fellowship International
Full Gospel Business Men's Fellowship International (FGBMFI) was founded by Demos Shakarian, a California dairy farmer. Shakarian's vision was to bring together businessmen from all denominations to network with each other and to share their faith in Christ. In contrast to CBMC, which had positioned itself in the noncharismatic evangelical stream, FGBMFI featured speakers from the charismatic healing revival stream of the day, such as Oral Roberts, Gordon Lindsay, Tommy Hicks and others who emphasized divine healing, speaking in tongues and demonic deliverance.

Full Gospel Business Men's chapters spread rapidly across the United States and eventually into 134 nations of the world. Membership grew to hundreds of thousands. Although the constituency was largely from the Pentecostal/charismatic camp, "the typical meeting, usually held in a hotel ballroom or a restaurant, was often a marked departure from the traditional Pentecostal meetings of the past."[10]

Tension with the Church

Both CBMC and FGBMFI acknowledged a high esteem for the local church. Most of their leaders were church members. However, both organizations lived in an ongoing tension between ministry in what I call the extended church, which they described as "business men," and the nuclear church. The fact of the matter is that these pioneers of workplace ministries perceived an inherent weakness in the local churches as they knew them. They felt that something was lacking in the outreach and evangelistic programs of their churches as far as the marketplace was concerned. The churches apparently lacked the necessary skills to contextualize the gospel for the business community.

CBMC and FGBMFI concluded that the most effective force for evangelism in the marketplace would not be pastors, but businesspeople. They also realized that even after businesspeople were led to Christ, most churches were ill-equipped to nurture these new converts in their faith. Ted DeMoss of CBMC explains,

> We always encourage [new converts] to begin attending strong, evangelical churches that stand for the Bible as God's Word and for Christ as the only way to God. However, I have seen on numerous occasions that because of something in a person's past, it may take him several weeks or even months before his is willing to go back to church—if in fact he ever attended previously.[11]

DeMoss' conclusion is that fellow businessmen, i.e. CBMC members, would potentially have better success not only at evangelism but also at follow-up than a pastor would.

Predictably, in the minds of many people, this inevitable development would position organizations like CBMC and FGBMFI as competitors of the local churches. This state of affairs was by no means intentional, but while there were and are exceptions to the rule, it could hardly be avoided across the board. Concerning FGBMFI, J. R. Zeigler observes, "Many of the traditional ministers from pentecostal denominations could not adjust to this new approach; and although it was stressed that FGBMFI was not a replacement for the local church, many pastors felt threatened by this open ecumenical fellowship."[12]

In the next chapter, I deal extensively with the gap between the extended church and the nuclear church. At this point, however, it is worthwhile taking note of where some of the tension began historically.

Serious Escalation

Although other significant workplace ministries, such as Fellowship of Companies for Christ and International Christian Chamber of Commerce, were founded in the 1980s, the serious escalation of the faith-and-work movement is largely a phenomenon of the 1990s. In fact, many of the leaders with whom I have spoken would locate the tipping point to have occurred around 1997 or 1998.

This raises an important question: Why would God begin to speak to the churches more strongly than ever before about the church in the workplace around 1990? My strong suspicion is that the timing is in direct response to the establishment of the biblical government of the church. Although I have said it once, let me reiterate that the decade of the 1980s saw the initial widespread recognition of the gift and office of prophet and that the decade of the 1990s saw the initial widespread recognition of the gift and office of the apostle. The church understood that it was "built on the foundation of the apostles and prophets, Jesus Christ Himself being the chief corner stone" (Eph. 2:20). My best estimate is that the Second Apostolic Age actually began in 2001.

With the government of the church now in place, it could be expected that God would begin to entrust to His people certain revelation that previously would have been premature.

Os Hillman, director of the International Coalition of Workplace Ministries, writes in his book *Faith@Work* one of the best descriptions of this movement that we have. Here are some excerpts (with a few updates) that show its serious escalation:

> [In 1990] we could identify only twenty-five [to fifty] formalized workplace ministries. [In 2002] we have identified twelve hundred organizations that seek to integrate faith and work [fourteen hundred in 2005].[13]

> [In the mid-1990s] only one conference on spirituality in the workplace could be identified, now there are hundreds.[14]

> There are more than 10,000 Bible and prayer groups in workplaces that meet regularly.[15]

> Pete Hammond, author of *Marketplace Annotated Bibliography*, states that by 2000, there were approximately 350 titles published about the faith-workplace connection, with the first books published in the 1930s. By early 2005, there were over 2,000 titles by Christians about the faith-workplace connection, some focusing on leadership and management and others speaking to issues faced by all Christian workers. Since that time, this trend has only increased, with more and more publishers entering this category.[16]

Speaking of books, I have purchased and read more than 100 books on this subject, which actually is a relatively small number compared with the roughly 288 books reportedly produced each year. I have listed mine in an annotated bibliography, which ends up displaying an amazing body of literature. Well over half of these books on my list have been written this side of 2000.

At the risk of offending some of my friends by omitting their work, I nevertheless feel that it would be a courteous service to many who are reading this book to offer my Top 10 list. I will do so alphabetically, in the order of the authors' last names.

- *Frontline Christians in a Bottom-Line World* by Linda Rios Brook
- *The Glory Returns to the Workplace* by Richard Fleming
- *The 9 to 5 Window* by Os Hillman
- *Lasting Investments* by Kent Humphreys
- *God@Work, Volume II* by Rich Marshall
- *Church on Sunday, Work on Monday* by Laura Nash and Scotty McLennan
- *Church That Works* by David Oliver and James Thwaites
- *Doing Business God's Way!* by Dennis Peacocke
- *Your Work Matters to God* by Doug Sherman and William Hendricks
- *Anointed for Business* by Ed Silvoso

The Thinking Evolves

I am going to overgeneralize a bit here, but I find it interesting to attempt to analyze the approximate chronological sequence of ideas concerning ministry in the workplace.

Many of the books written up to the 1960s reflected the view that the workplace was "the world." Believers were part of the church, and therefore they needed to learn how to be *in* the world, but not *of* the world. If absolutely necessary, they would make excursions into the world, especially to provide finances for the church, but they were to get back to the safety of the church as soon as possible. "Come out from among them and be holy" was their motto. These ideas projected a fortress mentality.

By the 1970s, the influence of CBMC and FGBMFI was beginning to be seen in books that exhorted believers to regard the marketplace as an evangelistic challenge. Christians began to recognize that God had placed them in the workplace in order to give them the opportunity to lead unbelievers to Christ.

The authors of a number of the books written in the 1980s began to analyze how Christian principles should influence believers in business. Some were urging Christian business owners to make whatever changes would be necessary in their businesses in order to reflect the best of biblical morality and ethics.

It was in the 1990s that many of the authors on the subject began to gain the understanding that what believers do in the workplace is a legitimate form of Christian ministry. This concept is a basic premise of this book as well. An interesting insight, which I also mentioned in chapter 1, is that work and worship are closely connected in Hebrew thinking. In fact, the Hebrew word *avodah* has a dual meaning: It means both worship and work. Leaning on this thought, David Miller founded The Avodah Institute in 1999 to help leaders integrate the claims of their faith with the demands of their work. The group is doing an admirable job (see www.avodahinstitute.com).

I will have more to say about work as ministry in due time, but meanwhile, I would like to highlight what I feel will be the cutting-edge of the literature on the faith-at-work movement in the 2000s. I have tried to reflect it in the subtitle of this book: "How God's People Can Transform Society." A major purpose of understanding work as ministry is to be an agent of God to take dominion, as I stressed in chapter 3.

The "Full-Time Ministry" Balloon

One of the principal blockages to the understanding that our work can be our ministry is the "full-time ministry" balloon that the church has persistently floated. This common idea presupposes that the ultimate goal of any believer who desires to please God fully is to go into full-time ministry as a pastor or a missionary or an evangelist or a Bible-school teacher or a worship leader or some other "legitimate" ministry position. Having to spend 40 hours a week on earning a living tends to be seen as God's Plan B for our lives.

The Overproduction of Seminaries
One of the causes of this unbiblical way of thinking is the persistent overproduction of traditional seminaries and Bible schools. Seminaries,

engaged in theological education, and Bible schools, engaged in ministerial training, are, by and large, designed to equip men and women for vocational nuclear-church ministry. This is the message they commonly send to their potential donors. They exist to help people get into God's Plan A for their lives, which is full-time or ordained ministry.

Nevertheless, a large number of graduates of these seminaries and Bible schools choose not to enter vocational ministry, so they end up somewhere in the marketplace. Many years ago, Fuller Seminary decided to present an alumnus-of-the-year award. I was teaching at Fuller at the time, and I was also an alumnus. I must have had a friend on the selection committee, because I turned out to be the person chosen. However, the committee was painfully aware that many other distinguished alumni couldn't qualify because they weren't in full-time ministry. So, facing this reality, they decided to make two awards, one for the church alumnus of the year and another for the marketplace alumnus of the year.

The marketplace alumnus was my friend Mel Schlueter, an attorney and also a trustee of the seminary. It occurred to me that Mel couldn't have made direct use of even 10 percent of what we had paid seminary tuition for in his law practice. The rationalization for his three years at seminary would, of course, be that they had built his Christian character. I say "rationalization" because, for one thing, donors did not expect that their contributions would be used to train lawyers—something they would consider to be God's Plan B. For another, who could conclude that Christian lawyers who had *not* spent three years in seminary would necessarily have characters inferior to those who had?

The Emotional Appeal of the Altar Call

Another cause behind the thinking that full-time ministry is God's Plan A has been the emotional appeal of the altar call to serve the Lord. Many nuclear-church leaders have received their personal call to vocational ministry through a special experience with God. So in order to minister to those in their churches or in their conferences, they attempt to create an emotional climate so that as many others as possible can receive the same call. They preach a message that locates vocational ministry as a missionary or a pastor on the top rung of the spiritual ladder. Then they invite those who at that moment feel they are hearing God's call to full-time service to go forward for prayer.

The reality of the situation is that a huge percentage of those who sincerely respond to the altar call never actually end up in vocational ministry. This experience, in many cases, will leave an emotional scar on those who find themselves in the workplace because they sadly feel that they have disobeyed God and are locked into living out God's Plan B for their lives.

All of this can produce a dysfunctional mind-set. Those who have graduated from seminary or those who have gone forward to dedicate their lives to full-time service and who do not end up in vocational ministry are subject to criticism and accusations. How often have we heard that such people "have given up their call" or "love the world and not Jesus" or "have turned out to be spiritual underachievers"? The worst accusation is that "they have decided not to go into the ministry," the implication being that ministry is done only in the nuclear church.

The False Distinction Between Clergy and Laity

The idea that ministry is only done in the nuclear church reflects the crippling distinction between clergy and laity. Even before I began to understand about workplace ministries, I suspected that there was something seriously wrong with distinguishing between clergy and laity. But probably because I had been so programmed with the Greek way of thinking, I was quite tolerant of the idea. Now, however, I see that it is counterproductive.

Rich Marshall agrees. He writes:

Two little words, words that misrepresent God and His plan, have been used by the enemy to bring about the development of a caste system within the Body of Christ—those who are called to "professional ministry" or "full-time ministry": the "clergy"; and those who are not: the "laity." It is my conviction that all of us in the Body of Christ are called to "full-time ministry."

When we allow this caste system to disturb our thinking, we create a problem for many who experience the strong call of God on their lives. We need a terminology and a mindset that works to eliminate the "second-class citizen" concept in the kingdom of God.[18]

Fortunately, as I have tried to show, we are now beginning to move strongly forward on the more positive pathway that Rich Marshall suggests. The proliferation of workplace ministries, especially now that we have entered the Second Apostolic Age, is helping to change our antiquated paradigms so that many of us, if not most, understand that God's Plan A is what we do six days a week in the workplace.

The New York Times

Who would think that Chuck Ripka, for example, is stuck with God's Plan B for his life?

I started this chapter with an extraordinary article from *Fortune* magazine. Let me conclude it with an equally extraordinary article from *The New York Times Magazine*. Again, it is a cover story, this time by Russell Shorto; it's called "With God at Our Desks: The Rise of Religion and Evangelism in the American Workplace." Although the article tells about much more, it features a man named Chuck Ripka.

In the article, Shorto reminds the readers that Jesus preached His message in the marketplace, where moneylenders were found; then he goes on to say this:

And so it remains. Chuck Ripka is a moneylender—that is to say, a mortgage banker—and his institution, the Riverview Community Bank in Otsego, Minn., is a way station for Christ. When he's not approving mortgages, or rather especially when he is, Ripka lays his hands on customers and colleagues, bows his head and prays: "Lord, I pray that you will bring Matt and Jaimie the best buyer for their house so that they have the money to purchase the new home they feel called to. And I pray, Lord, that you grant me the wisdom to give them the best advice to meet their financial needs."[19]

Russell Shorto has earned his stripes as an investigative reporter. Here is what he found after immersing himself in workplace ministries:

> [Chuck Ripka] is not literally a man of the cloth, but in the parlance of the initiated he is a marketplace pastor, one node of a sprawling, vigorous faith-at-work movement. An auto-parts manufacturer in downtown Philadelphia. An advertising agency in Fort Lauderdale. An Ohio prison. A Colorado Springs dental office. A career-counseling firm in Portland, Ore. The Curves chain of fitness centers. American Express. Intel. The Centers for Disease Control and Prevention. The I.R.S. The Pentagon. The White House. Thousands of businesses and other entities, from one-man operations to global corporations to divisions of the federal government, have made room for Christianity on the job, and in some cases have oriented themselves completely around Christian precepts.[20]

Ripka is far from being self-conscious or cautious about using business as a vehicle for evangelism. Shorto quotes one of the purposes of Ripka's bank, as stated in its annual report; it is to "use the bank's Christian principles to expand Christianity." "If that wasn't clear enough," writes Shorto, "Ripka put it in even starker terms for me: 'We use the bank as a front to do full-time ministry.'"[21] So much for clergy versus laity! So much for banking's being God's Plan B!

So how do Ripka and the Riverview Community Bank relate to transforming society? That, after all, is the theme of this book. *The New York Times Magazine* gives this report:

> Ken Beaudry, a marketplace pastor whose heating oil company is just down the road from Riverview bank, takes the same view: "It's about recognizing that we exist as a company not just to make profits, but to change society. And our employees are on board with that."[22]

Chapter 6

Two Cultures, Two Rule Books

By now I would imagine that most readers have come to the conclusion that there is quite a difference between the two forms that the church takes, namely, the nuclear church and the extended church. I'm sorry to report that this is a correct conclusion—there is quite a difference—and it's one that needs some analysis if we hope to stay tuned into what the Spirit is saying to the churches these days.

Consider, for example, what *Faith Today* magazine reports:

> If you took a poll of Christian business people, many would tell you that they love their churches. They love the worship and the people. Church is important to them, and so is their faith. But if you asked those people how their faith and church life relate to the barrage of decisions, stresses, and demands they face at their jobs on Monday, many would say, "It's not easy to explain."[1]

No, it is not easy to explain, because very few church pastors have been trained to relate the basics of faith to the world of the workplace. Probably 99 percent of seminary graduates never took a course on ministry in the workplace, and most never even discussed it in a single class session while they were in school. Seminary faculty members typically are not workplace people; they are nuclear-church teachers. In seminary, pastors are trained to minister to the personal needs of the people in their congregations, to offer spiritual advice, to explain the meaning of the Bible, to help parishioners live holy and righteous lives, to draw them to God in worship, to build relationships and fellowship, to deepen prayer lives and to enable people to use their spiritual gifts in church ministries. Most of them do this well. But, with a few notable exceptions, pastors have never had firsthand immersion in making their living from the marketplace, and consequently they do not have a backlog of experience to draw from when they preach or give personal counsel.

Quite the contrary. *Faith Today* goes on to say, "In some churches, people commonly express fears and suspicions about the marketplace. They talk about it as a dangerous place, where corporate greed, compromise, materialism, and workaholism conspire to undermine the spiritual lives of their parishioners."[2]

The Four Facts

Once we understand that there is a difference between the nuclear form of the church and the extended form of the church, four facts that have huge implications emerge. I use the term "facts" to avoid the impression that they might be figments of my imagination. No, these facts have been established by professional, social-scientific research. I previously introduced Laura Nash and Scotty McLennan, who wrote the book *Church on Sunday, Work on Monday*. They teach in respectable graduate institutions (Harvard and Stanford), they qualify for research grants, and they have carried out extensive research projects on the differences between the nuclear church and the extended church. They do not use those particular terms, but their phrases "church on Sunday" and "work on Monday" express the same thoughts.

These are the four facts, which I am extrapolating largely from Nash and McLennan's research:

1. Each of these two forms of the church, the nuclear church and the extended church, has a distinct culture. Some people might prefer to say that since both compose one church of Jesus Christ and both are part of the kingdom of God, that they, in fact, represent two distinct subcultures of the Kingdom. Either description will work.

2. The cultural gap between the two is enormous. I began to realize that there was a gap soon after I started reading the lit-

erature on the faith-at-work movement back in 2001, but I had no idea that the gap was as large as it is until I read *Church on Sunday, Work on Monday*. It turns out to be a wider gap than most people think. In fact, it assumes the proportions of the Grand Canyon!

3. Each of these two cultures (or subcultures) has its own rule book. This is simply Anthropology 101. Every human culture has its particular rule book. I will expand on this point later.

4. Most extended-church leaders know both rule books. They belong to local churches and attend them on Sundays. They are considered to be good church members because when they are in the nuclear-church culture, they follow the rule book of the nuclear church. And the other six days of the week, they operate effectively out of the rule book of the extended church. On the other hand, most nuclear-church leaders know only one rule book, the rule book of the nuclear church. They are almost clueless about the rules by which their church members function most of the time. Furthermore, and this is where trouble often begins, they tend to evaluate the lives and the behavior of their members by the standards of the nuclear church's rule book all seven days of the week.

It should go without saying that I have just described a scenario that creates the potential for several areas of misunderstanding (or conflict).

The Nature of Culture

Before I specify some of those areas of conflict, I'd like to look into the nature of culture itself. I do have some credentials to do this, since for 16 years I worked as a cross-cultural field missionary in Bolivia and, for 35 years after that, I taught missiology, or cross-cultural missions, on the faculty of Fuller Theological Seminary.

A simple way to begin to understand how cultures differ from one another is to think about baseball and cricket. Even though they are both played on an open field and involve hitting a ball with a stick and running in a certain pattern, they have different cultures. Each culture, of course, has its own rule book.

I know the baseball culture and rule book quite well. I earned three varsity letters in baseball in high school. I am familiar with technical rules, such as the infield fly rule. I know when a base runner is likely to steal a base. I know when the pitcher should issue an intentional base on balls. I can predict when a batter will bunt. I can see when the infield is in double-play position. When I attend a baseball game, I invariably keep score on every batter throughout the nine innings.

However, when I watch cricket on TV (I've never actually been to a cricket game), I find that I have a relatively short attention span. I see people throwing, hitting, running and catching, but it bores me. Why? Simply because I do not know the rules of cricket. I am not familiar at all with the cricket culture. I know that I could learn the rules of cricket if I wanted to, but for whatever reason, I don't want to. Even if I did, I realize that I would constantly be comparing the rules of cricket to the rules of baseball.

Cricket Is Stupid!

I recall that some time ago, when the subject of cricket came up, a friend of mine exclaimed, "Cricket is a stupid game!" When he did, I said (to myself, not out loud), *That statement is what is stupid!* Why? Neither baseball nor cricket is right or wrong; neither is stupid nor intelligent. They are simply different because they have different cultures. My friend obviously did not understand the nature of culture.

When I come to the subject of the faith-at-work movement, I do so as a nuclear-church apostle. All the books I have written before this one have been primarily from the point of view of the nuclear church. As a matter of fact, all the considerable body of literature on the current apostolic movement is focused on nuclear-church apostles, with a few recent exceptions, such as Bill Hamon's *The Day of the Saints* (which contains 82 pages on the ministry of apostles, prophets, evangelists, pastors and teachers in the workplace), Rich Marshall's *God@Work*,

Volume 2, and Os Hillman's *The 9 to 5 Window.*

I know the nuclear-church culture like I know baseball. And I also want to learn as much about the extended-church culture as I can, which I can't say about cricket. In fact, I think that I have already learned enough about the extended church to write this book and to begin to describe the rules of both cultures in order to highlight some of the important differences.

Cultural Similarities and Differences

Human beings, of course, have a huge number of characteristics in common. We all walk on two legs, chew our food before we swallow it, drink water, reproduce through sex and communicate by a spoken language. Most differences surface among humans who happen to live in different cultures. It is the same with the nuclear church and the extended church. The church of Jesus Christ requires the new birth for admission, submits to the authority of Scripture, worships God, exhibits the fruit of the Spirit and believes in the Resurrection. Differences surface, however, when we distinguish between nuclear-church culture and extended-church culture.

Cultural differences, in their purest form, are neither good nor bad. Unfortunately, every known culture has been corrupted to one extent or another by the sin of the human race and by demonic forces that have gained access. Nevertheless, behavior patterns by themselves are simply value-neutral rules that serve to bring order to society. Japanese, for example, eat with chopsticks, take their shoes off before going into the house, buy and sell with yen, and drive their cars on the left side of the road. Americans, on the other hand, eat with forks, leave their shoes on in the house, buy and sell with dollars, and drive on the right side of the road.

Which is right? The Japanese culture is right for Japanese, and the American culture is right for Americans. If Americans go to Japan, however, they will fare better by obeying the Japanese rule book. They might be forgiven for using a fork, but not for driving on the right-hand side of the road. So far, so good. But let's go on to think about international relations, where each party comes with his or her own rule book. Japanese, for example, have a gift-giving culture. For them, it is proper to give gifts to those with whom they hope to do business internationally. Many Americans, however, interpret such gifts as bribery or corruption or a kickback, especially when governmental agencies are involved. It is easy to see how legitimate cultural conflicts can develop.

When Do We Cut Slack?

I point this out because, as we look more closely at the rule books that distinguish nuclear-church culture from extended-church culture, we do well to avoid being overly judgmental. I realize that this principle is not always easy to follow when it comes to some interpretations of cultural norms. It's not always clear when we should be strict and when we should cut slack. Every culture, for example, has both written rules, such as laws and ordinances, and unwritten rules. They are of equal importance. I am not suggesting "situation ethics" or some sort of moral relativism, but I am attempting to point out that there can be legitimate, honest differences of opinion concerning appropriate cultural behavior.

To take a well-known apostolic example, recall the differences of opinion between Paul and Peter concerning eating with the Gentiles. Both knew the Old Testament law, and both wanted to please God. Paul's interpretation of the law gave him good reason to eat with Gentiles. Peter's interpretation gave him equally good reason not to eat with Gentiles. And as we know, they ended up with their share of misunderstanding and conflict (see Gal. 2:7-8,11-14).

We can apply this to something as obvious as traffic laws today. Through the years, I have driven in each of the 50 states, and I have found that the culture of different states interprets the written law in different ways. For instance, in every state, the written law says that pedestrians have the right of way. In California, this rule is taken literally, so when a pedestrian enters a street, even though not in a crosswalk, cars will stop. But not in Chicago! I recall that a friend of mine, who was a native Californian, was almost killed when he stepped into a Chicago street for the first time. The same is true for stop lights. The written rule in all states is that motorists do not go through a red light. Again, Californians obey this law. But not in Colorado, where it is common practice to push the limits of the yellow light and occasionally not quite make it through before the light turns red. In Colorado, when the light turns green, it is wise to first look both ways to make sure that the cross traffic is stopping before you go.

Feelings Run Deep

Peter Tsukahira, a Japanese-American who is now a pastor and a businessman in Israel, sees things like this in the church-marketplace cultural conflict. He explains, "Culture contains values and expectations that lie beneath our conscious thoughts. There is a church culture and there is a business culture. Although the two coexist in the believing community, it is as if they have different values and goals, speak different languages, and have entirely different customs."[3]

Feelings can run deeper than we may think. Here is how Paul Gazelka, a Christian businessman whom many consider a marketplace apostle, expresses it:

> In many Christian circles there is a definite two-tiered system of ministry importance, sometimes described as "clergy" and "laity." Clergy are the called ministers, and lay ministers merely help them minister. Lay ministers are like apprentices of a trade that can never graduate to the next level. As a marketplace minister, I've occasionally felt the condescending attitude from well-meaning professional ministers of the gospel who hold this view. At times I've felt like what minorities of any culture must have to overcome to accomplish their roles in an environment that is sometimes full of prejudice.[4]

Perhaps it is because I am a professional missiologist that I have sensed a special assignment from the Lord to clarify these cultural rule books as much as possible. In the second part of this book, I list and describe some of the rules themselves. But I feel that it would be good to first be sure that we understand more of how wide this Grand Canyon between nuclear-church culture and extended-church culture really is.

In order to do that, once again I am going to draw on Laura Nash and Scotty McLennan's findings.

Attitudes of Workplace Believers

First, let's look more closely at the attitudes of workplace believers, as reported by Nash and McLennan:

> Congregants in business who said they felt very close to pastors on issues of family, personal well-being, or community outreach told us a different story when it came to their role as business-people. Here they often felt ignored, disdained, or simply beyond the comprehension and experience of most clergy.
>
> One man's comment is quite representative: "You have to expect the clergy to haul you over the coals a little. Otherwise, why would you go to church? To be told you're doing everything right? But when you hear this stuff, it's just so off base. They don't understand what business does. It's such a turn off!"[5]

Nash and McLennan reported this statement from another believer in the workplace:

> I love the Church, but sometimes I look at what we do in the company, the nonprofits we work with, the family policies, and I believe in many cases we [business] have found a more effective vehicle for these concerns *outside* the church. I begin to wonder, you know.[6]

Nash and McLennan conclude that the attitudes these believers have could be boiled down to these statements:

- The clergy are the last people to go to for guidance on business.
- They don't understand the issues.
- They can't manage themselves; how could they advise others?
- They hate business.

- They're jealous of people with money.
- They want to criticize business but they have no problem with accepting its money.
- It's not their role to comment on business.
- We don't speak the same language.[7]

Attitudes of Clergy

Clergy stand tall on the other side of this Grand Canyon. In fact, since they understand only one of the two rule books, most clergy don't even realize that the Grand Canyon exists. Here is some of what Laura Nash and Scotty McLennan have written on this topic:

> Indeed, many clergy reported that they felt ignored or simply powerless to have a significant impact on businesspeople, but they did not know why. They would assume, for example, that businesspeople were simply too greedy or indifferent to care about real spiritual issues, and that the predominance of a market mentality in society was simply overwhelming the flock.[8]

> Comments about money usually led to comments about culture, which strongly influenced people's values. In fact, clergy used the term *culture* as a shorthand symbol for what they felt is the root of the problem: a value system centered on money. The culture, they told us, is a materialistic, hypercommercial place, worshipping money above all else.[9]

Unspoken Thoughts

Most clergy sincerely want to minister to the businesspeople in their churches. Their calling is to care for the entire flock. The previous quotes from clergy reflect, more than anything else, an underlying frustration at the persistent disconnect they have with certain marketplace leaders. They largely keep this frustration to themselves until researchers like Nash and McLennan begin to ask questions that draw them out of their attempted denial.

If I am not mistaken, there are also some unspoken thoughts, not to mention fears, on the part of many clergy. Even in response to objective research, they would hesitate to verbalize these feelings, but at least in many cases these three unspoken thoughts are more than bothersome:

1. *An ownership issue.* Clergy are well aware of the choleric temperaments, the self-assurance, the leadership skills, the desire for excellence and the compulsion to succeed that characterize many businesspeople in their congregations. They are equally aware of their own weaknesses in some of those areas. The question that they begin to ask themselves is, *Will they take over my church?* In response, the clergy, often unwittingly, begin to build in safeguards to see that such a thing doesn't happen.

2. *A control issue.* This relates to the concept that there might be a legitimate form of the church out there in the workplace. It is difficult for some nuclear-church leaders to accept this idea because, if they do, members of their congregation may begin to minister in leadership roles as apostles, prophets, evangelists, pastors and teachers in the extended church, where traditional nuclear-church leaders have little spiritual authority. If the only church is the nuclear church, the ordained clergy can maintain some control. But if not, they begin to wonder, *Will I lose control? Could some of my church members position themselves under an additional spiritual authority?*

3. *A money issue.* This thought can go through the minds of pastors: *If I begin to equip workplace leaders and encourage them to minister in the extended church, they might think that they need to use a good deal of their financial resources to finance the ministry opportunities that open up for them there.* In the minds of the workplace leaders, these extracongregational opportunities might seem more important than the activities on the budgets of their local churches. The question that pastors begin to ask themselves is this: *Will I lose their tithe?*

A Clergy-Dominated Church

Consider how Paul Anderson sees this picture. Anderson is the leader of the Lutheran Renewal movement. He is a second-generation renewal leader, having succeeded well-known author Larry Christensen in his position. Soon after he took over, he concluded that the efforts to renew the entire Evangelical Lutheran Church in America (ELCA) from the inside were, to all intents and purposes, futile. So he started working with renewed ELCA congregations that desired to move their allegiance to a new network called ARC (Association of Renewed Churches) under the apostolic leadership of Anderson.

Keep in mind that, at the time of the Reformation, Lutheranism distinguished itself by rediscovering the doctrine of the priesthood of all believers. In other words, every believer had direct personal access to God without consulting a professional priest. However, Lutherans did not seem to be able to move from the *priesthood* of all believers to the *ministry* of all believers, as we will see here.

Anderson points out that the official Lutheran doctrine of the definition of the church is this: "The church is where the Word of God is preached and the sacraments rightly administered."[10] But he then goes on to suggest what he considers to be a deficiency of this definition. Anderson writes, "This definition falters most profoundly as it highlights the role of pastoral professionals to the exclusion of the so-called laity."[11] Behind this comment is the fact that in the Lutheran Church, the only ones authorized to administer the sacraments rightly are the ordained clergy, to the exclusion of those who are leaders in the workplace.

Anderson continues:

> In today's clergy-dominated church, we have trouble trusting lay people. They may fly 747s, or oversee multinational corporations, or teach in the classroom, but often we are reluctant to release them into meaningful roles in the church . . . Even the language of the institutional church is imposing: pastors "preside" at communion and they "officiate" at baptisms. Make no mistake; these are power words, conveying the concept that

certain priestly duties are exclusively for the spiritually elite and specially ordained.[12]

Two Rule Books

Anderson lists some very crucial questions that this issue raises: "Why do non-ordained people frequently doubt their own calling and effectiveness? Why do they typically defer ministry to the experts? Why do they often feel unqualified, dumb, and fearful of failure?"[13]

In light of what we have been saying, these questions most likely reflect the fact that there are, indeed, two rule books. The Lutheran Church is by no means alone in defining ministry according to the rules of the nuclear-church rule book. Most other denominations do the same. But workplace people are more than aware that the picture is larger. They know both rule books, and they have a heartfelt desire that their pastors appreciate the extended-church rule book as well as the nuclear-church rule book.

I believe that this process will be greatly facilitated if some of the rules are defined well enough so that their differences can become mutually understood, not as right or wrong, but simply as different, cultural behavior patterns. The balance of this book will attempt to advance that process.

Part 2

The Two
Rule Books

Introduction to
the Rule Books

By this time, I would hope that readers will have agreed that there are indeed two legitimate forms of the church, the nuclear church and the extended church, and that each one of these forms has its own culture and its own rule book.

Laura Nash and Scotty McLennan observe that "businesspeople and clergy live in two worlds. Between the two groups lie minefields seeded with attitudes about money, poverty and the spirit of business."[1] Not only do they live in two different worlds, but also theirs has not always been a peaceful coexistence. Words like "minefields" raise the specter of misunderstanding, hostility and conflict. This is a scenario that we must avoid at all costs. I interpret it to be a defensive tactic of the enemy.

As I have strongly suggested, God's will is that we, His people, move forward as an army to transform the societies in which we live. We are commanded to take dominion. The title of Eddie Long's book on this subject is *Taking Over*. Taking over what? Taking over the territory that Satan has dominated since Adam and Eve forfeited their God-ordained dominion. Satan is alarmed that God's people are so vigorously tooling up for a huge offensive against his kingdom of darkness. Little wonder that he would make a last-ditch attempt to divide God's people so that he cannot be conquered.

The Land and Cosmic Forces

To refresh our memories, I will reproduce once again our social-transformation graphic, this time with two additions, namely, the land and cosmic forces. These are the two areas calling for intense spiritual warfare. We must not underestimate our enemy's power or be blindsided by his tactics.

Cosmic Powers

Social Transformation

The Church In The Workplace	Workplace ← Apostles →	The Transfer of Wealth
The Government of the Church		Breaking the Spirit of Poverty

The Land

The entire schematic rests on the land. Society cannot be transformed without dealing aggressively with the pollution of the land, which Satan has been able to produce throughout eras of human history. We are in an excellent place now because, for more than a decade, God has been revealing strategies for redeeming the land, strategies that, by and large, the Body of Christ had been previously unaware of.

It is beyond the scope of this book to begin to detail the ways and means that we now have to break the curses of blood and corruption and covenant breaking that stain much of planet Earth and that provide legal grounds for Satan to accomplish many of his hateful and ungodly desires. However, I feel it is necessary at least to place the issue of the land on our agenda for taking dominion. Suffice it at the moment to recommend two of the most outstanding books that we now have as a result of 15 years of research, experimentation, field work, consultation and hearing from God. They are *Informed Intercession* by George Otis, Jr., and *Releasing Heaven on Earth* by Alistair Petrie.

Overarching the whole diagram are cosmic forces. Ephesians 6:12 reads, "For we do not wrestle against flesh and blood, but against principalities, against powers, against the rulers of the darkness of this age." Social transformation involves spiritual warfare on the highest levels. We will make no progress unless we take seriously the mandate of God to address these pernicious forces of evil. The apostle Paul explained that the purpose of his ministry was that "the manifold wisdom of God might be made known by the church to the principalities and powers in the heavenly places" (Eph. 3:10). That is the purpose of our ministries as well. If we don't do this through the power of the Holy Spirit, the enemy will attack the different components of the schematic one by one, attempting to disjoin them so that God's people will be neutralized in their efforts to fulfill the divine mandate to take dominion.

Again, instead of elaborating, I will simply refer readers to three of the best current books for details on what God has been showing the Body of Christ concerning strategic-level spiritual warfare over recent years: *Possessing the Gates of the Enemy* by Cindy Jacobs, *Shaking the Heavenlies* by Ana Méndez and *Authority to Tread* by Rebecca Greenwood.

The Minefields

Going back to the minefields, if the church in the workplace is going to flourish and if God's people are going to transform society, the minefields must be cleared. The leaders of the nuclear church and the extended church must move forward shoulder to shoulder. Leaders of both forms of the church must be open-minded about understanding and appreciating where each group is coming from. Kent Humphreys has done a remarkable job of promoting this understanding in his book *Lasting Investments*. It is a guidebook for pastors and other nuclear-church leaders who wish to take concrete steps in closing the gap between the two worlds. His subtitle says it all: *A Pastor's Guide for Equipping Workplace Leaders to Leave a Spiritual Legacy*. A second excellent book that focuses on the responsibilities of those in the extended church is Os Hillman's *The Faith@Work Movement*. Many people regard Os

Hillman as having the most knowledge about the different aspects of this whole field.

In my opinion, the best way to negotiate the minefields is to know what the mines are and where they are located. The mines are related to the cultures and the different rule books of the nuclear church and the extended church. If the rules of the one culture are misunderstood or ignored by leaders of the other culture, the mines will explode. But, on the other hand, if the rules of each are known and understood by the other, the mines can be defused.

In the remainder of this book, I give brief descriptions of eight of these rules and mention four others, showing how they compare and contrast in both rule books. This is definitely a risk. To my knowledge no one has done this up to now. The major fear that I have is to be misunderstood by nuclear-church leaders. Most of them, as I have pointed out previously, have been ministering for years under the assumption that theirs is the only rule book and that deviations from it are to be corrected. My approach is that most of the deviations are indeed legitimate behavior patterns for the extended church. Particularly those who tend to see issues in black and white without wide areas of gray between them are likely to wonder if I am teaching so-called situation ethics.

Godly Ethics

No, I am not teaching situation eithics. I believe in biblical holiness. I agree with Peter Tsukahira, who says:

> Believing businesspeople will face temptations to compromise their ethical standards that the average pastor does not face. Corruption in business is a fact of life. . . . The average businessman or woman needs superior ethical standards and godly wisdom to function in the business world with excellence. God has too few servants in business whom He can trust with large sums of money and the freedom to associate widely in a business environment.[2]

Drawing on my background as a missiologist, I see my task as defining these rules as best as I can. My approach is phenomenological. It is not philosophical or theological or exegetical or revelational, all of which are legitimate, alternative approaches that many of my good friends regularly take. I am simply trying to focus more on what *is* than on what *ought* to be.

If I am successful, the minefields will be safer, and we, God's army, can move forward harmoniously toward transforming the societies in which we live.

Rule 1

Ministers in
the Workplace

Kent Humphreys accepted Jesus as his personal savior when he was nine years old. From that point on, he consistently desired to deepen His relationship with Christ and to serve God with his whole life. His personal spiritual growth of course took place in the nuclear church and under the nuclear-church rule book.

The Spiritual Ladder

What understanding of the ministry of the church did Kent obtain? If he really wanted to serve God, what should he plan to do with the rest of his life? What rules did he learn in church? Now a businessman, Kent writes:

> I was forming a picture of what life would look like to those who truly have their lives committed to God. I saw the Christian life as a type of ladder. On the top and best rung of this ladder, the rung reserved for the most committed, were the missionaries, and God sent them overseas. On the next rung were the preachers and pastors of this world, followed closely on the next rung by vocational church staff. Farther down the ladder came workers in Christian organizations, and somewhere down near the bottom was a businessperson.[1]

Robert Fraser, a successful businessman and currently chief financial officer of a large prayer ministry, has expressed similar feelings in his book *Marketplace Christianity*.

> There ought to be a symbiotic relationship between business leaders and the church. Business leaders should enable and empower the church with their gifts. The church should help leaders understand and wholeheartedly pursue their purpose in life. There should be a healthy overlap between marketplace and the church, each supplementing and breathing life into the other. Yet the church often doesn't know what to do with its business leaders. They sit in pews like priceless, untapped resources. If churches knew how to draw out that resource, they'd discover that strong leadership exhibits and produces vision, unity of purpose and selflessness.[2]

Pastors Don't Know Any Better

The root of the problem that Kent Humphreys and Robert Fraser are describing, of course, is that nuclear-church leaders have not been trained to understand the rule book of the extended church. Their nuclear-church rule book assumes that all Christian ministry is done in the context of the local church and that what is done out in the workplace is just "work," not ministry. This should not be judged as a character flaw on the part of pastors. They simply don't know any better.

However, businesspeople who do know both rule books predictably end up frustrated. For example, one businessperson says, "[The church leaders] always ask me to head the finance committee, and of course I am able to give a large donation. But that's about all they understand about my role as a businessman: I can do the books. In their eyes, when I'm doing what I do at work, I'm not a real person with a real soul."[3]

My personal theological and ministerial training indoctrinated me in the nuclear-church rule book. According to that rule book, where do believers do ministry? In the church. Period. I am embarrassed to admit, now that I am aware of both rule books, that for most of my ministry, I taught that a believer's spiritual gifts should be used in their churches and that they did not apply to what a person did in the workplace.

Spiritual Gifts in the Workplace

As a matter of fact, if someone were to ask me what I feel was my most significant contribution to the Body of Christ over my 50-plus years of ordained ministry, I would say that it was my teaching on spiritual gifts. My textbook, *Your Spiritual Gifts Can Help Your Church Grow,* has remained in print for 30 years. Here is the way I define a spiritual gift: "A spiritual gift is a special attribute given by the Holy Spirit to every member of the Body of Christ, according to God's grace, for use within the context of the Body."[4]

The obvious question that arises is, What do you mean by "in the context of the Body"? My traditional thinking (which, of course, I have now changed in the newest edition of the book) was that the Body was the local church or local-church outreach programs or parachurch ministries or something of the sort. People would often ask me directly whether I thought that their spiritual gifts were given to use in the workplace as well as the church, and I, regrettably, would say no. In the earlier editions of the book, I quoted Baptist professor Jack MacGorman to reinforce my position: "Not only are the gifts *functional,* but they are also *congregational*" (emphasis in the original).[5] Then I went on to say, "Most of the things God does in the world today are done through believers who are working together in community, complementing each other with their gifts in their local congregations."[6] How wrong I was!

No one has helped me understand ministry in the marketplace more than my friend Ed Silvoso. In his book *Anointed for Business,* Silvoso argues that the spiritual gifts that God gives us apply "primarily to the marketplace."[7] I am now a bit amused to admit that, even though Silvoso's opinion is 180 degrees different from what mine used to be, I now fully agree with him. He has enabled us to grasp some of the implications of the extended-church rule book.

For example, Silvoso brings up Mark 16, where it says that believers will heal the sick, cast out demons and overcome serpents, among other things. He then points this out:

> The context for Jesus' words is the command, "Go into *all the world* and preach the gospel to all creation" (Mark 16:15, emphasis added). The process described by Jesus is *definitely* centrifugal and expansive. The entire world, the totality of creation, must be the focus of the mission entrusted to us, not just a church building or a gathering of believers.[8]

Equipping the Saints

I have said a great deal about apostles in this book. It is important to keep in mind that, according to Ephesians 4:11-12, the explicit primary task of apostles (as well as of prophets, evangelists, pastors and teachers) is to equip the saints for the work of the ministry. These saints are not just those who have church or parachurch jobs, such as pastors or music directors or cell-group leaders or conference speakers or Sunday School teachers or choir members or deacons. That would add up to only about 20 percent of the saints.

Rather, the work of the ministry is to be done by 100 percent of believers. What does that mean? It means that we don't do the work of the ministry just one day a week when we are in church but that we do it seven days a week. What we do in the workplace Monday through Saturday is true ministry. Believers who are bus drivers or farmers or corporate CEOs or electricians or television producers or elected government officials or school teachers or stay-at-home moms or newspaper reporters are all doing ministry. This is what the extended-church rule book teaches.

Is this, what I am calling Rule 1, biblical? Yes, it is. The New Testament Greek word translated as "ministry" is *diakonia*. However, it is translated as "ministry" only about half the time. The other half of the time it is translated as "service." The amazing conclusion that we can draw from this is that whenever we are serving someone else, we are doing biblical ministry! Think about this. If you are filling someone's teeth, you are ministering to your patient. If you are playing in a symphony orchestra, you are ministering to the audience. If you are flying an airplane, you are ministering to the passengers. If you wait on tables, you are ministering to the customers. If you sell auto insurance or if you lay carpet or if you work in the accounting office or if you coach little league, you are ministering. All of that clearly fits under biblical *diakonia*.

A Job Versus a Ministry

What is the difference, then, between a job and a ministry? A job becomes a ministry when God leads you into your area of work and you take the voice of God, the anointing of God and biblical principles into that area as you work and minister.

An excellent book dealing with ministry according to the extended-church rule book is Laura Nash's *Believers in Business*. In researching the book, she interviewed more than 85 evangelical Protestant CEOs. Here is her conclusion:

> [They] seemed to have a *deep personal meaning about work itself*. Fred Smith has a nice phrase for it: "My work is my worship." His claim is not simply a mechanistic acting out of Christian ethics; it goes much deeper to the creation of an unbroken link between the *process* of working in the world and fulfilling one's personal identity as a Christian.[9]

The spiritual gifts that God has given to each and every believer are part of one's identity as a Christian (see 1 Cor. 12:18). The extended-church rule book opens the way for the saints of God to use their gifts and to fulfill their God-ordained destiny through fruitful ministry wherever they may spend the majority of their time.

Rule 2

Apostles in
the Workplace

The groundwork for this rule regarding apostles in the workplace was laid in chapter 2. I do not desire to be redundant, but I couldn't imagine attempting to list and describe the rules of the nuclear church against the rules of the extended church without going back to the subject of apostles.

Two Forms of the Church

For the benefit of those who have not digested chapter 2, I will summarize the chapter. The true church exists in two forms, the nuclear church (congregations) and the extended church (workplace). Since they are both the true church, it would be expected that both would be built on the same governmental foundation, namely, apostles and prophets (see Eph. 2:20). A great deal of work has been done in recent years on the nature and ministry of nuclear-church apostles, but very little has been done on extended-church apostles.

In other words, the nuclear-church rule book is becoming quite clear on the gift and office of apostle, while the extended-church rule book on apostles is still in the beginning stages of formation.

Let's keep in mind that my overall purpose is to address what I consider to be a major word from the Lord to the churches today—that of social transformation. The graphic that depicts our paradigm has the bar of social transformation supported by two pillars: the church in the workplace and the transfer of wealth. The dynamic connection between the two is workplace apostles, not nuclear-church apostles. My personal conclusion is that without the overt ministry of workplace apostles, neither the gate to the transfer of wealth nor the gate to significant social transformation will ever be opened as wide as God intends them to be.

A Growing Consensus

We can be encouraged by a growing consensus among Christian leaders that there are indeed apostles in the workplace. In 2000, Bill Hamon wrote, "It is more than likely that God has already placed true apostles throughout the marketplace. They have not been that effective in their ministries, however, because they have not been recognized for what they are."[1] In 2002, Ana Méndez predicted their arrival: "We will see apostles in the financial world rise up, men and women filled with the glory of God and with divine passion."[2] And as I have already mentioned, in 2005, Rich Marshall outlined some of their characteristics.[3]

By focusing on apostles in this rule, I do not mean to leave the other governmental offices of the church out of the workplace. For example, Bill Hamon explains that the business sphere contains God-anointed fivefold ministers:

> Apostles are like the founders or entrepreneurs who launch divisions of God's enterprise on planet Earth. Prophets are like strategists who plan and evaluate how to meet Kingdom objectives. Evangelists are the sales managers who inspire their team to expand the business. Teachers may be likened to trainers who ground the workers in the principles, products, and services of the organization. Pastors are similar to local business managers of units or branches who oversee the regular operations of their people, encourage them to meet their full potential, and help them work together as a team.[4]

It will not be easy for many nuclear-church leaders to admit that God has placed these gifts and offices in the extended church as well as in the nuclear church. As soon as they do acknowledge this though, the question then arises as to whether these workplace leaders should be ordained or commissioned into their offices. They never went to seminary to learn Greek and biblical exegesis and hermeneutics and homiletics and systematic theology and church history as "normal" ordained ministers do. They haven't been called to "full-time Christian work," as the nuclear-church rule book would refer to it. "What right would they have to be recognized as Christian leaders on our level?" some nuclear-church leaders would ask. Little wonder why most pastors, denominational executives and ministry leaders would hesitate to go where this road seems to lead.

Apostles and Their Spheres

While all of the offices mentioned in Ephesians 4:11 will need to be activated in the extended church if we are to see society literally transformed, apostles are key. They are the forerunners. Taking dominion of society in the name of God is first and foremost a spiritual battle, and apostles are the generals of God's army, so to speak. John Kelly writes this description: "Warfare is the number one role of the apostle. Prophets will woo you with the Word of the Lord; teachers will educate you; pastors will help you through your problems and hurts; evangelists will get folks saved; but it is the apostle who will declare war on the enemy and lead the Church to war."[5]

If apostles in the extended church will lead the warfare to transform society, what are the battlefields on which they will fight? This question comes up from time to time in the faith-at-work literature. Ed Silvoso frequently pinpoints three, namely, business, government and education.[6] I used to have a list of 16. Bill Hamon enumerates the battlefield as well:

I believe there are apostles of finance, technology, medicine, industry, education, the military, government, law, communications, business, transportation, nuclear science, agriculture, and a hundred other segments of society.[7]

Hamon's list is 13 plus 100! Most of these lists are random thoughts that come to the minds of the authors as they're making a point.

We all agree that the society to be transformed is not just one big conglomerate, but a unified whole that is made up of several vital pieces, each one of which must take its own path toward transformation. These segments of society should be seen as apostolic spheres. Apostles have authority, but limited authority. They only have authority in their God-given sphere. Paul reflects this when he "boasts" of his authority (see 2 Cor. 10:8), but then qualifies it when he goes on to say, "We, however, will not boast beyond measure, but within the limits of the sphere which God appointed us" (v. 13).

The Battlefields

If we are planning strategy for war, it would be advantageous for us to agree on the battlefields. My suggestion is that we standardize our terminology, using a list that can be traced back to Loren Cunningham, founder of YWAM, and Bill Bright, founder of Campus Crusade. In 1975, Cunningham wrote down seven chief categories of society and put the list in his pocket. He states:

> The next day I met with a dear brother, the leader of Campus Crusade for Christ, Dr. Bill Bright. He shared with me something God had given him—several areas to concentrate on to turn the nations back to God! They were the same areas, with different wording here and there, that were written on the page in my pocket. I took it out and showed Bill. Amazing coincidences like this happen all the time when Christians listen to the still, small voice of the Holy Spirit. . . . These seven spheres of influence will help us shape societies for Christ.[8]

This was first brought to my attention by business consultant Lance Wallnau. He calls them the seven mountains. The warfare strategy is that "if the world is to be won, these are the mountains that mold the culture and the minds of men. Whoever controls these mountains controls the direction of the world and the harvest therein."[9] This involves confronting the principalities and powers that control the high places at the top of each of the seven mountains. The real spiritual warfare is up at the top. Wallnau wisely says, "Satan is well aware that a single Mao or Stalin or Hitler is a greater agent in his quest for global domination and destruction than a thousand Anton LaVeys."[10]

Wallnau not only calls these determinative social components mountains, but he also calls them mind molders. Cunningham calls them spheres of influence. Bright sees them as areas of concentration. Bill Hamon calls them segments of society. I would like to propose that we all get on the same page and agree to call them the seven molders of culture.

The Seven Molders of Culture

1. Family
2. Religion
3. Government
4. Media
5. Education
6. Business
7. Arts

Each of the seven molders of culture obviously would have any number of significant subdivisions. That is where Bill Hamon's "hundred other segments" will fit. Each should be seen as an apostolic sphere, requiring apostolic leadership to transform that unit into a society that reflects the values and lifestyle of the kingdom of God. Not only that, but consider the fact that each of these molders of culture and each significant subdivision will have its own rule book. Only those who are immersed in the culture of that social unit will understand the rule book and know how to operate by its rules. They are the only ones who will be able to change the power structure at the top of each mountain.

Nuclear-church apostles can influence religion and, to a degree, family. But they have virtually no influence over the other five molders of culture. Only extended-church apostles will be able to lead the army of God into those strategic battlefields. Lance Wallnau asks, "How do we go about reclaiming the mind molders of nations, and what does this have to do with you and your calling to the marketplace? Everything! You are about to be drafted into an elite unit of marketplace commandos."[11]

Then Wallnau goes on to suggest a battle plan:

> Look at your occupational field and see it as a mountain. What companies and people are at the top of that mountain? Why are they at the top? What skills, knowledge, and personal characteristics are needed to occupy that position? What would need to exist for you to occupy the top of that mountain?[12]

I love that challenge!

CBS Loses a Battle

Let's look at the area of media for an example of what is needed to bring about change in the workplace. Linda Rios Brook has a notable reputation as a manager of commercial television stations. She is one who points out the relative impotence of nuclear-church-based attempts to bring change in television programming. Brook tells this story:

> In my years in network television, I have seen many picket lines, letter-writing campaigns, and attempted boycotts by Christian organizations in protest at the abysmal decline of standards in programming pumped into the living rooms of America at all hours of the day. For all the energy and rhetoric invested in demanding a response, I have seen only one success by any organization where a major programming

decision was reversed as a result. This singular success did not come about by Christian clout, but rather by political fervor and fear of financial consequences.[13]

Linda later goes on to say, "My conclusion, after witnessing hundreds of failed campaigns, is many Christian organizations refuse to be educated in the weapons of warfare in the marketplace."[14] Another way of putting it would be that nuclear-church leaders are operating out of a rule book that is irrelevant in the workplace.

What then is the answer? "Until workplace ministry advances," writes Brook, "and we have successfully seeded the centers of power and decision making with believers, we will never be successful in implementing change on the basis of our moral or religious conviction."[15] This means that we need a biblical government in the workplace. It takes a government to overthrow a government.

What was the one success that Linda Rios Brook, who happens to be a member of the International Coalition of Apostles, had seen? It involved CBS and a program that would have been very damaging to Ronald Reagan and his family. The change in programming did not come because of nuclear-church pressure. The power centers of corporate America do not care much what Christians think. Brook explains, "They do, however, care very much about law and buying power. This is why in November 2003, a politically motivated and perfectly orchestrated campaign of protest successfully persuaded the management of CBS to pull a highly controversial program concerning the Reagans from its prime time schedule."[16]

Why couldn't the nuclear church make something like this happen? It is because they are following a different cultural rule book. Here is the difference: "The currency of the entertainment industry is not moral conviction or religious fervor. It is cost of sales, earnings per share, and legal leverage. Traditional church leaders, typically, do not know how to navigate these waters, but Christian businesspeople do."[17]

This leads us to Rule 3.

Rule 3

Influence and
Authority

What, more than anything else, distinguishes an apostle from other members of the Body of Christ who have been given other gifts? This is an important question. It is like asking what it is that distinguishes a nose from other parts of the human body, because the Bible relates the distribution of spiritual gifts, like the gift of apostle, to the differentiation of body parts (see 1 Cor. 12:14-18). The answer to the second question is, of course, that the nose smells. Likewise, an apostle is distinguished from others in the Body of Christ by extraordinary authority.

Where does this authority come from? Both the nuclear-church rule book and the extended-church rule book agree that it comes from God. For example, the apostle Paul writes to the Corinthians that he would not be ashamed to "boast somewhat more about our authority"; then he immediately adds, "which the Lord gave us" (2 Cor. 10:8). God is the One who decides which believer is to receive which spiritual gift (see 1 Cor. 12:11), including the gift of apostle.

But let's begin to think how this God-given authority is recognized and confirmed in the nuclear church as opposed to the extended church. While the two rule books have the same starting point, authority, they soon diverge from one another in significant ways.

Relationships Versus Respect

The key word describing the pathway to influence in the nuclear church is "relationships." The key word describing the pathway to influence in the extended church is "respect." Nuclear-church leaders are programmed by their rule book to level the playing field as much as possible. Their view of humility causes many of them to be embarrassed if they are considered to be above their peers. "After all," some would say, "we are all the family of God; we are all sinners saved by grace; we must not think of ourselves more highly than we ought to think; and pride comes before a fall." This is institutionalized, for example, in Australia through what many church leaders whom I know call the tall-poppy syndrome. If one person, in his or her own mind, grows taller than those around, the proper thing is to cut this person down to size. To the Australians, relationships trump assertive leadership.

Things are quite different out there in the workplace. In that rule book, respect is the starting point, even for potential relationships. Workplace leaders hesitate to relate personally to others until they pass the test of respect. Take, for example, *Business Reform* magazine, one of the prominent periodicals for extended-church leaders. The editors, naturally, try to design their covers in such a way that readers will turn to the material inside. They also know that, in their culture, the more the authors of the articles are respected, the more readers will be attracted. Therefore, it is not surprising to see a cover with a picture of David Green of Hobby Lobby with the headline, "Hobby Lobby is a $1 Billion Empire." Likewise, another issue carries a cover picture of John D. Beckett with the ID: "Owner of $100 Million Beckett Companies." It would be hard to imagine a cover like that on *Christianity Today* magazine!

It is not a coincidence that both of these respect-building journalistic lines in *Business Reform* carry dollar signs. A chief goal of those in the marketplace is to make money. Those who make a lot of money tend to gain more respect than those who do not. Peter Tsukahira affirms, "In a real sense, businessmen today are the stewards of modern civilization. Those without money serve those who control it."[1]

The Gift to Produce Wealth

Speaking of spiritual gifts, Paul writes to Timothy, "Do not neglect the gift that is in you" (1 Tim. 4:14). In Timothy's case, it was most likely the gift of evangelist (see 2 Tim. 4:5). In the business world, however, the gift that needs to be stirred up in the lives of many believers could well be the gift to produce wealth. Deuteronomy 8:18 says, "You shall remember the Lord your God, for it is He who gives you power to get wealth." Just as Billy Graham likes the public to know how many people respond to his evangelistic invitation on a given night, so David Green likes the public to know that Hobby Lobby is worth $1 billion.

Unfortunately, many who are following the nuclear-church rule book would judge Billy Graham's report as reflecting spiritual power, while they would judge David Green's report as reflecting sinful pride.

The research of Laura Nash and Scotty McLennan has surfaced an important contrast in the views of authority between the two rule books. They acknowledge that both groups claim authority from God, but then they go on to say this:

> The sources of the groups' authority obviously differ. The businessperson acquires authority largely from past success . . . and present affiliation with power. The pastor acquires authority from more diverse sources: on the one hand from the congregation; but also from the hierarchical, bureaucratic systems of the academy and their denominational authorities.[2]

Wealth Changes History

If we continue to focus on social transformation, or taking dominion, as our ultimate goal in accomplishing God's purposes here on Earth, it is important to recognize once again that, throughout human history, three things above all have changed the course of society: violence, knowledge and wealth. And the greatest of these is wealth. Why? It is because wealth carries with it proportionate influence and authority. Businesswoman Megan Doyle argues that the economy controls today's society. It controls political elections and foreign policy. "Because of this," she says, "the leading business people in our culture are the ones who hold the most authority in our society."[3]

Building on this, I recall a conversation I had with Megan in Minneapolis a few years ago. We were talking about influence and authority, and at that time I did not yet understand much about the extended-church rule book. She said words to this effect: "Peter, I know many pastors throughout our state. Unless I am mistaken, I don't think any of them could call their senator in the morning and expect to have their call returned by the afternoon. But I can. The reason is not that I am more spiritual than they are; it is because I am rich!"

My knee-jerk, nuclear-church-rule-book mental reaction was, *Wait a minute. Who does she think she is? Is she serving Mammon rather than God?* But fortunately, the Holy Spirit stopped me short and super-imposed this more sensible reaction in my mind: *Wait a minute. I've never heard anything like this before. This woman knows something that I don't know, and I want to learn what it is as soon as I can.* The upshot was that Megan became a strong mentor for helping me understand the things I am now writing about in this book.

However, many nuclear-church leaders would still strongly object to remarks like Megan Doyle's, for they are not yet aware of the extended-church, prosperity mind-set. Ed Silvoso observes that

> the Church widely, although perhaps unintentionally, teaches, or, at least, implies that God despises rich people and that success is something Christians cannot handle well. . . . Unfortunately, when it comes to the social divide between the rich and the poor, the Church often exhibits a negative bias toward the rich, the result of ascribing innate virtue to poverty while suspecting intrinsic vices in wealth.[4]

Money Mind-sets

Where does the nuclear-church rule book derive the practice of "ascribing innate virtue to poverty," as Silvoso says? Back in chapter 4, I traced the spirit of poverty in our churches today to medieval monasticism. I think it would be accurate to say that the nuclear-church rule book advocates a *monastery mind-set* while the extended-church rule book advocates a *prosperity mind-set*. No wonder misunderstandings arise at times.

Two of the individuals who would undoubtedly make an imaginary *Time* magazine list of the 100 most influential Christian leaders over the 2,000 years of church history would be St. Francis of Assisi and John Wesley, one a Catholic hero and the other a Protestant hero. I fully agree that they should be on the list. I greatly admire the lives and the character of both of them. In fact, I recommended that we all follow John Wesley's advice on giving, which I spelled out in chapter 4. However, these two spiritual giants, as well as many others like them, were major contributors to the monastery mind-set of the nuclear-church rule book.

The Monastery Mind-set

St. Francis was born into an affluent family. His father ran a successful import-export business. However, when he was 24, Francis renounced his inheritance. In a public ceremony, he took off all of his clothes and gave these elegant garments back to his father. As the Bishop of Assisi saw Francis's dramatic gesture, he placed his cloak on him. From that point on, Francis wore a simple garment made of flax with a cord around his waist. According to the National Shrine of Saint Francis of Assisi, this "solemnized his 'wedding' with his beloved spouse, the Lady Poverty, under whose name he surrendered all worldly goods, honors, and privileges."[5] Legend has it that when Francis died, he even removed his simple cloak and was covered with only a borrowed cloth in order to keep his vows with Lady Poverty until the end.

John Wesley also held poverty in high esteem. Though his income rose higher and higher throughout his life, he lived with the bare necessities and gave the rest to the poor, among whom he lived and ate. In 1744, he wrote, "When I die if I leave behind me ten pounds . . . you and all mankind can bear witness against me, that I have lived and died a thief and a robber." In 1791, when he died, the only money referenced in his will was a few coins in his pockets and dresser drawers.[6]

Don't these stories make you stand in awe of the two men's wonderful dedication to God? But don't they also make you feel that if you don't do something like that from now on, you might be letting God down? These legitimate heroes of the faith are legendary role models, and the implicit conclusion is that every believer should be like them, at least to the extent possible. It is easy to see where the monastery mind-set came from and why many nuclear-church leaders, to this day, equate poverty with piety.

The Prosperity Mind-set

Neither St. Francis nor John Wesley has been looked to as a role model for most extended-church leaders. Their rule book, in fact, dictates a *prosperity* mind-set. One workplace leader I know said to me, "It's true that money isn't everything, but it's right up there with oxygen!" Rich Marshall affirms the importance of money for gaining influence:

> We need to start thinking about authority outside traditional interpretations—and not just who can exert authority, but the tools that go with it. For example, consider money. For years, especially in the church world, it has borne the image of "filthy lucre." Yet, money is a tool God gives to businesspersons to gain authority in their city.[7]

Extended-church apostles love Jesus' story of the 10 minas in Luke 19. In this story, a rich man gave 10 servants a mina each (about $5,000) to trade while he was gone. When he returned, one of these servants reported that the 1 mina had become 10 minas. The master then said, "Well done, good servant; because you were faithful in a very little, have authority over ten cities" (Luke 19:17). How do you get influence over a city? One way, according to Jesus, is by being a good trader and obtaining wealth. I know that in my city, the wealthiest people are the most influential. The poor people are not running my city, make no mistake about it. The same is probably true of yours.

Rich Marshall sums up this rule well:

Marketplace Ministers [or extended-church apostles] must operate outside of conventional nuclear church models. . . . For years we have attempted to reach cities by means of nuclear church programs, outreaches, church planting, unity efforts, prayer movements, and every other conceivable local church concept. Yet when Jesus speaks of authority in the city, He is referring to the impact that comes from businesspeople doing business. I am confident that when Marketplace Apostles are recognized for who they are, we will see new strategies and actions that will result in major, beneficial changes in cities and nations of the world.[8]

Rule 4

Time **Management**

Back in 2001, the year that I was just beginning to get acquainted with workplace ministries, our pastor went away on a trip; he asked a businessman, who was a member of the church, to take the pulpit the Sunday he was gone. When I saw who was going to preach, I tried to think of the last time this had happened. I could remember businessmen giving the pitch for Gideon's International, the Bible distributing agency, and laypeople giving testimonies of how God had worked in their lives, and finance committee chairpersons making appeals for funds. But this time, a representative of the extended church was in charge of the whole sermon!

His assignment was simply to tell the congregation what he did in the business world to serve the Lord. I loved how down-to-earth he was. It was a relief to hear someone in the pulpit who wasn't using religious language. He wasn't preaching to us, but he was an excellent communicator. He was accustomed to leading large sales meetings and motivating employees. He was upbeat because he was very successful in his businesses. We knew we had a winner in the pulpit! I enjoyed his talk as much as anything I've heard in a Sunday-morning church service

Skipping Church to Make Money

I don't remember too many of the details of the content, but one thing he said I have not forgotten. Throughout the talk he had many good things to say about our pastor. At one of those points, he shared words to this effect: "The pastor and I get along well. For one thing, he doesn't scold me when I don't show up at church. The reason is that he knows and I know that when I'm not here, I'm out there doing what God has called me to do—I'm making money!"

This was a very unusual thing to hear from a Christian pulpit. Fortunately, it wasn't out of synch with the church I belonged to at the time because the senior pastor, Ted Haggard, happens to be one of the possibly 5 percent of American pastors who understand both rule books, the nuclear-church rule book and the extended-church rule book. The other 95 percent of pastors, however, are programmed to one degree or another with the monastery mind-set that I described in Rule 3. To their way of thinking, someone's making money instead of worshiping God on Sunday would be better admitted in the confessional rather than in the pulpit.

My suspicion is that numerous believers who are businesspeople, but who are at the same time members of the 95 percent of American churches that I just referred to, have exactly the same thoughts, but they check them at the door on Sundays. They are accustomed to switching from one rule book to the other. They respect their pastors and they know that their pastors would never agree with putting material things ahead of spiritual things, so they simply don't bring it up. And consequently, they're worried about what the pastor thinks when they don't show up at church. If they were ever able to preach, they would never mention that they play hooky from church from time to time.

Greek Priorities

Somehow or other, the infamous Greek mind-set that I described in the first chapter has entrenched itself in the thinking not only of church leaders but also of many Christian workplace leaders. Remember the Greek dualism, which separates "form" from "matter" or, in the church, separates "spiritual" things from "worldly" things? Work, of course, both for Greek philosophers and for many Christian pastors, fits into the worldly category. On the other hand, the Hebrew mind-set would see everything, including going to work and going to church services, as equal parts of life under God. Don't forget, the Hebrew word "avodah" means both work and worship.

Many respected Christian workplace leaders, whose books I have read, take for granted that life should be prioritized around three priorities: first God, second the family, and third work. Ironically, some of them, in the same book, decry Greek thinking and commend Hebrew thinking. Strangely, it has not occurred to most of them that their priorities are derived from none other than Greek thinking.

This explains why many pastors would not hesitate to criticize a businessman who is a church member for deciding that on a given Sunday, making money (working) is more important than going to the church service. They have their priorities wrong.

The Nuclear-Church Calendar

The nuclear-church rule book includes a weekly calendar. It varies from church to church but, with the exception of Seventh-Day Adventists and a few others, the Sunday morning worship service is the nonnegotiable meeting for anyone who wants to be considered a faithful and obedient believer. After that, the more committed Christians will find a way to show up at meetings like Sunday School or a Sunday-evening service or a Wednesday-night prayer meeting or a small-group or church social functions. And those who are even more committed will agree to serve on church committees or boards and will show up for those meetings. The point I am making here is that all of the above, good as they might be, require *time*.

David High, for example, learned the nuclear-church rule book in the standard way, by attending a Bible school, serving on a church staff, doing mission work, teaching in Bible school and leading home Bible studies. He planted a church and pastored it for years. Then suddenly, God called him to the marketplace, where he started operating under the extended-church rule book. He writes, "Talk about culture shock. Suddenly all the clichés and statements of faith I had laid on the men of my church were tested in the arena of reality."[1]

High soon found out how difficult it was, as a businessperson, to live up to the expectations that he used to have as a pastor. He explains:

While a pastor, I had little appreciation for the difficulties men had in running businesses, leading their families, while at the same time trying to support all the ministries and programs of the church. When I pastored, I wondered why men didn't come Tuesday night for choir practice, Wednesday nights for Bible study, Thursday nights for evangelism, and Saturday mornings for prayer. Now that I was one of those businessmen, I never seemed to be able to work it into my schedule either.[2]

Many workplace saints who have 9-to-5 jobs and who do not carry work responsibilities home with them can easily accommodate the nuclear-church rule book, and they do. However, those in the extended church who are leaders or professionals of various kinds, which would include most workplace apostles, usually carry work responsibilities home with them and have much more of a struggle with time management.

Feelings of Guilt and Condemnation

The dilemma that workplace leaders constantly face is well-described by Peter Lyne in his book *First Apostles, Last Apostles*:

I'm thinking especially of people whose primary calling is in the realm of business or some specific career. Often they prove to be apostolic figures, who need all the encouragement and support that we can give them. What they don't need is to be left on the fringe of church life, with a feeling of guilt and condemnation, because they can't be at many of the meetings or participate in all the projects. The demands of their role frequently make it difficult for them to be more involved in the day-to-day life of the church.[3]

Businessman and publisher Gregory Pierce strongly expresses his feelings from the point of view of the extended church:

It never ceases to amaze me how insensitive many church professionals are to this problem. While they are encouraging people to spend more time with their families and spread the Good News in the workplace, many think nothing of allowing or even encouraging people to volunteer five, ten, even twenty hours a week. In fact, in much the same way that businesses reward workaholics, religious institutions tend to praise and reward "churchaholics" for their overinvolvement at church.[4]

Because these church members have skills that many of the others don't, most pastors would like to have them on their church boards and in their business meetings. According to the traditional, nuclear-church rule book, businesspeople have the opportunity to do "ministry" by serving their church. The nuclear church hasn't yet comprehended the truth that a person's work is a ministry on the level of being a member of the church council. Some businesspeople indeed are called by God to invest the time required to serve as members of church boards, but others are equally called by God to do other things, such as make money. Neither, in itself, is more spiritual than the other.

Church Business Meetings

Peter Lyne recognizes that the conflict that Christian businesspeople experience extends to church business meetings:

> The average church business meeting leaves anyone with a modicum of intelligence wishing they were somewhere else. Business people, used to making decisions and shaping strategies, get completely frustrated with the pernickety details that some well-meaning folk delight in bogging everyone down with! The Church still manages to promote a dualism between the sacred and the secular that is completely misleading, leaving so many talented people with a second-rate feeling and nowhere to go.[5]

To make this more personal, consider David Oliver. As a marketing professional, his primary guide has been the extended-church rule book. At the same time, he is deeply involved with not just one church but many of them as a church consultant. Of meetings in the business world, Oliver writes:

> In the real world, where time is costed and weighed up in its use, meetings are quite interesting. I have just come from one of my clients this morning. We had a meeting of seven highly-paid men and women. We started at nine-thirty and by eleven I had finished the minutes. We had twenty-five action points—most of these will be actioned by the next time we meet, in another month's time.[6]

This is the way that the normal extended-church culture operates day after day.

Contrast that with the way that the nuclear-church culture tends to operate quite comfortably. Oliver describes a nuclear-church meeting like this: "The average church elders' meeting—four to six hours a week, with a budget a fraction of my client's. And if my experience with church audits is anything to go by, raising the same issues week after week, month after month, and even year after year!"[7]

Pew Potatoes

Workplace leader, how would you like to be called a pew potato? That's what happened in a church that Gregory Pierce once belonged to. An appeal was given for church members to sign up for church-ministry positions, and 61 people signed up. The headline in the next newsletter read, "Pew Potatoes Lose 61 to Parish Ministries." This did not go over well with businessman Pierce. He writes:

> What struck me was the assumption that anyone who was not volunteering for the parish was lazy and wrong—likened to a "couch potato" who does nothing but sit around and

watch television. But what if among some of those nonvolunteers there was a business owner who was working overtime to save a company and its fifty jobs, or a man or woman who was sandwiched between two generations and caring for both, or someone who was running an important political campaign, or somebody who was just plain "burned out"? And when they don't volunteer, do they really deserve to be labeled "pew potatoes"?[8]

Time management may not be the widest gap between the nuclear-church culture and the extended-church culture, but it clearly is one of them and is important to be aware of.

Rule 5

Stewardship

As I've been writing this book, I have become aware that I've been writing about money more here than in anything else I have previously written. As I mentioned in chapter 4, I lived most of my life oppressed by what I now identify as the spirit of poverty. Because of that, the attitude of businesspeople concerning money blindsided me when I began to concentrate on the church in the workplace. Fortunately, Bill Hamon broke the influence of that demonic spirit over me, which freed me to see in a positive light the new things I was learning from the extended-church rule book.

There was a time when my attitude would have interpreted what I have been learning about money as exploitation, greed, destruction, selfishness, materialism, worldliness, carnality and pride. Obviously, I was well-trained in the nuclear-church rule book.

The Cultural Gap

This rule concerning stewardship deals directly with money. For that reason, this could potentially turn out to be one of the most uncomfortable rules. The gap between the culture of the nuclear church and the extended church is quite wide at this point.

One who sees this gap as clearly as anyone is Mark Greene. Greene knows both rule books because he first had a career in advertising in the business world before he studied theology in seminary and then taught seminary students. He now leads the London Institute for Contemporary Christianity. Greene feels that much of the theology underlying what I am calling the nuclear-church rule book is flawed when it comes to attitudes toward the creation of wealth.

Greene writes in his book *Supporting Christians at Work*, "Many people who create wealth often feel that the church is deeply suspicious of wealth creation and judgmental about those involved in it."[1] He quotes a business ethicist who says:

> I sometimes wonder whether Christians [who follow the nuclear-church rule book] really do believe that material creatures are good or whether there is an eternal Manichee in many of us which considers the world and its contents eternally bad; an eternal dualism which considers material things and their production, marketing, and consumption, as not just inferior, but as positively alien to Christians.[2]

"[One] consequence of this non-biblical anti-materialism," continues Green, "is that the laity can easily be made to feel guilty about having money and about spending it on things that bring pleasure."[3]

The extended-church rule book, in contrast, considers making money a bona fide form of Christian ministry. Jesus is a prime example. As a carpenter, He may have made furniture or ox yokes or door frames for money. When he did a miracle and filled a boat with fish, the commercial fishermen who were with him sold the fish for money. Both activities involved making a profit.

I was once discussing this with a businessman friend of mine, Dan Meylan. He said, "Peter, let me give you a corporate principle. If you don't create a profit, you don't have a ministry." When I asked him what he meant, he said, "Part of corporate stewardship is providing for the well-being of the people who work for the owner. Without a profit, you cannot do it." Dan was addressing the extended church's rule of stewardship by pointing out that serious stewardship involves making money.

The Storehouse

The book of Malachi says, "Bring all the tithes into the storehouse, that there may be food in My house" (Mal. 3:10). One of the most obvious and most troublesome differences between the nuclear-church rule book and the extended-church rule book involves the understanding of what "storehouse" means. There is little difference of opinion as to whether believers should tithe, giving the first 10 percent of their income to the Lord. And there is also consensus that we should give additional offerings above the tithe. Both rule books agree on that point. (Implementation, however, is another question. George Barna's research indicates that fewer than one of ten born-again churched Christians in America actually tithe.[4] But that is a different matter.)

The disagreement comes in the decision as to where these tithes and offerings should be directed. Most pastors would argue that today's storehouse should be the local church. Bill Hybels, for example, says:

> It may be helpful to ask these questions when determining where to give. Where do I receive my primary spiritual feeding? Where do my children receive nurturing, care, and teaching? Where would I turn for help in a crisis? Where do I use my spiritual gifts? The answer to these questions should be, and usually is, the local church.[5]

Ralph Moore and Alan Tang agree: "The house of God is the place where we feed our souls. It is the spiritual warehouse that supplies our nourishment on a regular basis. A local church constitutes this warehouse, and God asks that we support it with a tithe."[6]

Some pastors even take this to an extreme and teach their people that what they give to the church should not be designated for certain ministries, such as "missions" or "feeding the poor" or "evangelism," because once people give their money to God, they should let go of it and not try to manipulate it. The subtle implication, of course, is that pastors are the ones who should decide where money is spent, not parishioners.

Many pastors become very upset when church members who make a substantial amount of money start their own charitable foundations, give their tithe to the foundation and make their own decisions as to how their tithe money should be spent. This, in the minds of such pastors, violates the rule of the storehouse.

It is true that many, if not most, extended-church people have also believed that the local church is the storehouse, and this is where their tithe has gone for years. Others, however, have not. Wolfgang Simson testifies:

> Those rejected, undiscovered or underemployed apostles and prophets suffer from what I call the "church trauma," a very deep and tricky wound inflicted on them by the very institution of healing, the church, which did not live up to it own calling. . . . Many of those Christian businessmen therefore heavily support anything but the church, investing in "parachurch" ministries and "missions."[7]

Statements like this come as disturbing news to pastors, especially to those who have been ignorant of what I have called the Grand Canyon between the workplace and the traditional church. But the statements are true. I recall talking to one businessman who had a strong heart for evangelism. I asked him about giving to the local church. "Give to the local church?" he replied. "For every $1,000 I give to the local church, few or no souls are saved. But if I give the same $1,000 to India or China, hundreds of souls will be saved!" When I asked him about the storehouse, he said, "Heaven is my storehouse. That's where Jesus told us to lay up treasures."

Limits to the Tithe

In a different vein, and this obviously would apply to only a small segment of believers, if extremely affluent individuals tithed to the church they belong to, the church could actually be hurt by it. One rich friend of mine said to me, "Peter, if I tithed my income to my local church, it would ruin the church." He and his family belonged to a small church that had a small budget and was pastored by a good man with a small vision. It was a fruitful match spiritually, but not financially. Whenever the church had a special need, such as a new building, my friend would give the first 10 percent of the cost, but nothing more.

I shared this story a while ago with Ted Haggard, who pastors a church of over 10,000, and discovered that he is in tune with the extended-church rule book at this point. He said that his policy has been that no church member should give more than 10 percent of the church budget or more than 10 percent of a special project such as buildings. I mention this to encourage other pastors who might not have thought of it in this way.

If businesspeople feel that they are giving the proper amount to their local church but they have additional funds to give for their tithes and offerings, where should they give them? A substantial majority give them to parachurch ministries of their choice. Some nuclear-church leaders endorse this, while others oppose it. Some, in fact, see the local church as the central organizational structure of the kingdom of God. They see parachurch ministries as God's Plan B. Plan A, in their view, would be that nuclear churches should be carrying out the functions of parachurch ministries, but because nuclear churches have defaulted, parachurch organizations are acceptable as a stopgap measure.

I have a different point of view. I happen to think that parachurch ministries are just as much a part of the church of Jesus Christ as are local churches. Donating to a parachurch ministry, therefore, is donating to the church.

However, which rule book do parachurch ministries follow, the nuclear-church rule book or the extended-church rule book? The fact of the matter is that they are in between. They function as nonprofits in many of the same ways that for-profit businesses function, except that some of them unfortunately have retained the nuclear-church, monastery mind-set, which I attribute to the spirit of poverty.

I don't expect that we will soon have total agreement between nuclear-church leaders and extended-church leaders on the rules of stewardship, but I do believe that the more we understand each other, the less disruptive our differences will turn out to be.

Rule 6

New Forms of
the Church

Just under 100 percent of the membership of a typical local church are workplace people. I realize that this is a truism, but I want to bring it to the surface of our minds as we begin to look at this rule.

In fact, the nuclear-church rule book goes beyond this observation and teaches that all those who are truly born again and committed to Christ should validate their commitment by being responsible members in a local church. In the face of this, noted researcher George Barna, who has been studying changing attitudes concerning American church membership for years, has been publishing statistics that show that this nuclear-church rule is being increasingly ignored or violated by born-again Christian adults. He calls this the Revolution, which also is the title of one of his newest books.

The Nuclear-Church Rule

In order to test this with a real-life nuclear-church leader, Barna shared his research findings with Harry, "an older pastor of a mid-sized congregation . . . [who] was a deep thinker and a devoted churchman."[1] Harry was visibly upset by Barna's suggestions that there might be new legitimate church forms. He said:

> You see, George, God has no Plan B. The local church is God's Plan A, His chosen vehicle, and He does not need any other plan. Anything outside of that is simply indefensible from a biblical standpoint. Never second-guess God, my

friend. Follow Him and accept His paths. No church has ever been perfect, but that's no reason to abandon it. Remaking the church into the form you desire, rather than the form God ordained, is simply not legitimate. Let God be God. Help the local church be more effective, but don't ever, *ever* take steps to replace it.[2]

A significant number of American Christians would beg to disagree with Pastor Harry. Recognizing that, *Charisma* magazine recently published a revealing article, "When Christians Quit Church." The article points out that this phenomenon is "a growing trend that is alternately worrying and exciting church leaders, pointing to what is being seen as either a serious threat to the spread of the gospel or the actual cusp of a revolution that could usher in the sort of revival many have prayed for and dreamed of for years."[3]

Church Dropouts

The article was bold enough, but I am not sure that the *Charisma* editors were prepared for the huge quantity of letters that they received in response. It is important to keep in mind that those who wrote were not ex-Christians, but rather believers who were regular readers of a decidedly charismatic Christian magazine. Five of the letters were from nuclear-church people who wrote things such as, "Don't be deceived! God wants you in His church. Satan wants you out."[4] Thirteen letters were from dropouts no longer following the same rule book. Most of them felt elated that a prestigious magazine would give them the privilege to speak their mind. Here are some of the quotes:

I was wondering if I was the only one! I've decided to leave traditional church settings because I am sick of the traditions of men and the "bless me" mentality.[5]

Sermons are shouted at the crowd, and the basic theme is to build the church's membership and keep people tied up one to three nights a week in church-based ministry. I feel God wants me to minister through my work.[6]

[My wife and I] are two of the Christians who are missing from church on Sundays. . . . People aren't leaving out of rebellion or sin. They are leaving because they need more spiritual input, and these churches aren't providing it.[7]

I love God and study His Word, but I don't see much point in going to church.[8]

I will continue to serve God, my family and the body of Christ with a whole heart. Will I go back to church? That remains to be seen.[9]

The *Charisma* readers who wrote these letters, along with many more like them, are workplace believers. They are choosing to follow the extended-church rule book at this point. One man wrote, "I feel God wants me to minister through my work." He is applying the Hebrew concept of avodah, linking work with worship.

Statistically, how many people are we talking about? George Barna did some significant research on unchurched adults, meaning those who had not been to church in the previous six months, except for special occasions. Many of these unchurched adults were born-again Christians. Barna writes, "Rechurching this group alone [i.e., born-again dropouts] would swell Sunday morning attendance by more than 15 million people. . . . That inflow would constitute the largest return to the Church during any decade in the past century and would increase the size of the average Protestant church by almost half!"[10]

Lack of Time and Interest

Why did these 15 million believers decide to leave their churches? Barna concludes:

We found that the dominant reasons for their avoidance of the church are lack of time and lack of interest: these two motivating factors cover about three out of five of the unchurched believers. Very few of these people stay away because of bad past experiences (less than 5 percent); more often, they duck the church because of irrelevant past experiences.[11]

The next question: Is this trend likely to continue? From what we know, the end is not in sight. In 2003, Barna found that the lowest church attendance of any age group in America was among twenty-somethings (31 percent). More than 50 percent of teenagers attend church. But there is a startling 58 percent decline in church attendance from age 18 to age 29. That would mean that there are something like 8,000,000 twenty-somethings who regularly went to church as teenagers but who will drop out by the time they are 30.[12]

It is fair to assume that not all of these church dropouts have lost their Christian faith or that they have lost their desire to serve God all their lives. The majority of them are seeking something that they have not yet found. Here is an interesting prediction based on current trends. In 2000, 70 percent of Americans saw the local church as their primary means of spiritual experience and expression, with only 5 percent located in an alternative faith-based community. However, by 2025, it is expected that only 30 to 35 percent will find their spiritual fulfillment in a local church, while the same number, 30 to 35 percent, will affiliate with an alternative faith-based community.[13]

Creative Alternatives

Another term for "faith-based communities" is "new forms of the church," the title of Rule 6. Many workplace believers who have given up on the traditional church structure are seeking creative alternatives for nurturing their spiritual lives and becoming better equipped for ministry. Linda Rios Brook says:

Marketplace ministers build new things and they fix broken things. They don't understand bureaucracy in the church and they will not jump through its endless hoops. They are willing and happy to work through the organization of the church so long as it does not prevent them from carrying out "their ministry." In which case, they will go around the church structure and do what God has placed on their hearts to do. They respect the clergy but consider many in the clergy to be naïve and ineffective at getting anything done.[14]

Comments like this, reflecting the extended-church rule of developing creative alternatives to the traditional form of the church when necessary, is obviously disturbing to most nuclear-church leaders. However, it is a fact of current life, and if nuclear-church leaders choose to be in denial, their effectiveness will be lessened.

A fascinating example of how this is happening comes from China, where modern Christianity is only about 30 years old. *Phoenix,* a Chinese magazine, reported that:

A Third Church, belonging neither to the Three Self official system nor the rural-based house church, is rising rapidly in major cities. Their members are mostly well-educated, urban professionals, including doctors, engineers and scientists. Many artists and writers are joining the Third Church. Even officials, in one city, are active members of the Third Church.[15]

This is a workplace church led by workplace ministers with a rule book different from the others. Such alternatives are opening the door for infinite creativity, not only in China, but also around the world.

House Churches

Here in America, the most widespread creative alternative to the traditional local church is the house church. Larry Kreider, who is a nuclear-church apostle but who is actively promoting this new church form, announces, "It is happening again. A new species of church is emerging throughout North America. In major cities as well as rural areas, a unique kind of church life is peeking through like the fresh growth of new crops pressing through the surface of the soil."[16]

Krieder's organization, DOVE Christian Fellowship International, is a worldwide network of cell-based churches and house churches. The subtitle of his book *House Church Networks* is *A Church for a New Generation*. Kreider believes that the twenty-somethings who have dropped out of traditional churches will increasingly be attracted to this new church form. He explains:

Hungry for community and relationship, people are learning the values of the kingdom by first-hand participation. They meet in small groups in homes, offices, boardrooms or restaurants. For them church has become a way of life where discipleship and growth occurs naturally as everyone develops their gifts and "learns by doing," under the mentorship of spiritual fathers and mothers.[17]

Where did the house-church movement in America come from? Businesswoman Linda Rios Brook has this perceptive insight:

It may or may not be coincidental that the rise of the home church began at approximately the same time the home school movement began. Both began for the same reason: a general dissatisfaction with what institutionalism had to offer and a belief that their children were at risk. Both began in similar ways. Neither had a champion. They arose from the grassroots of America. Neither asked permission nor announced their plans to any prevailing authority.[18]

Some of the other creative alternatives that are emerging include the following:

• *I-Church*. I stands for "Internet." Some traditional churches are now live webcasting their services so that parishioners can attend via their computer screens. For example, T. D. Jakes of The Potter's House in Dallas broadcasts his services to 3,480 viewers per month. A more advanced form of I-church is to conduct full-fledged church services interactively as does Argentine Sergio Scataglini. His church, ComunioNet, based in Indiana, serves congregants from Argentina, Spain, Peru, Uruguay and Mexico. Scataglini says, "This is real church. Every step of the church can be fulfilled through the Internet. We baptize believers and take communion together."[19]

• *Free-enterprise cells*. Although based in a traditional church, free-enterprise cells allow workplace church members to link meaningfully with unbelievers in the workplace around any topic of mutual interest. Ted Haggard at New Life Church in Colorado Springs originated this creative alternative to the standard home cell group, and it is catching on in growing numbers of churches. The marketplace cells are allowed to function under their extended-church rule book. Haggard's blueprint for free-enterprise cells is found in his book Dog Training, Fly Fishing, and Sharing Christ in the 21st Century.

• *Corporate churches*. Corporate churches, or workplace churches, are groups of believers working for the same organization who have established a form of church in their workplace. They might, for example, obtain permission to use a room in their workplace facility on Thursday nights. The employees, with their families, meet there, worship, share God's Word, fellowship, counsel, pay their tithes, take communion and do whatever else is expected in church. For most, this is the only church with which they are affiliated. One corporate church parishioner said to me, "A great advantage of our church is that we can give 90 percent of our church income to missions." He, of course, was referring to the fact that they had no expenses for facility or church staff as do most institutional churches.

I have no doubt that other new forms of church could be added to this list and that any number will continue to appear in the future. I don't believe they will ever replace the typical, traditional church form that we have known. I remember the days when people opposed televising football games because they thought it would empty the stadiums. It never has and it never will. There is something about being with a large congregation of like-minded fellow believers under the leadership of a pastor and having programs for children and youth, loud corporate worship, visibility in the community and the fellowship of the saints that appeals to most Christians, myself included. I don't want to be a church dropout. I could not imagine going to church on a computer monitor!

Having said that, however, I would also like to say that I have great respect for those who find alternative forms of church appealing. I love the nuclear-church rule book on Sunday mornings, but since many of my brothers and sisters in the Lord have tastes different from mine, I also want to be open to affirm them and to give them the freedom to use as many creative alternatives for new church forms as God leads them to do.

Rule 7

The Means
and the End

Let me pose a question that everyone has heard many times: Does the end justify the means?

The knee-jerk, politically correct response to this question is, "No, of course not. The end can never justify the means!"

Can the End Justify the Means?

But let's give the question some more thought instead of just giving a rote answer. When you think about it a bit, the correct answer to the question has to be "Certainly the end justifies the means. What else could possibly justify the means except the end?"

For example, my lawn needs mowing. That is the end. In order to accomplish the end of mowing my lawn, what means do I use? I use a lawn mower. I don't use a rototiller or a snow blower or a pressure washer or a chainsaw or a pair of scissors or an antique grass scythe, all of which I happen to own. Why not? Because none of these means would be suitable to accomplish my end.

Or suppose I need to go to a one-day meeting in Dallas. My time is very limited. I live in Colorado Springs. I need to get from the Springs to Dallas and back. That is the end. What means do I use? I decide to fly. I don't drive a car; I don't start up one of my four wheelers; I don't take the Greyhound bus; I don't hitchhike. Those means of transportation would not be the best to accomplish my chosen end. Further, I decide to fly directly to Dallas. I could fly through Atlanta or through San Diego or through Chicago, but I choose none of those means because of my limited time. On what basis do I make such decisions? Only on the basis that the end justifies the means!

Here's a scenario that relates more directly to the marketplace: You have $150,000 to invest. Your goal, or your end, is to use it to earn 20 percent over the next year. What are the possibilities? Stocks, bonds, commodity futures, foreign exchange, venture capital, savings accounts, hedge funds, money market, real estate and more. How do you make your choice among all these investment vehicles? You choose the means that will best accomplish your end.

I would imagine that, especially on that last example, some readers are beginning to have second thoughts, because making money is not like taking an airplane or mowing your lawn. Ethical issues could easily arise in financial transactions. Some means for making the 20 percent, such as stealing it or gambling or marketing pornography or padding expense accounts or dealing drugs, could not be justified simply because they could accomplish the end. For that reason, the axiom "The end doesn't justify the means" certainly applies in ethics class. That the end does not justify unethical or immoral means is a sound, ethical principle. But beyond that, it is largely irrelevant to most of our lives in the real world, because day in and day out we choose means that will best accomplish our ends.

Pragmatism, Is It Worldly?

The reason I have belabored this point is because it precipitates one of the widest gaps between the nuclear-church rule book and the extended-church rule book. The issue is pragmatism. I personally know a great deal about this because I am, by nature, a pragmatic person. I am a choleric, High D, type A personality. If I have a job to do, I tend to do whatever it takes to get it done as quickly, as efficiently and as effectively as possible. I am aware that in this regard, I follow the extended-church rule book more than the nuclear-church rule book, much to the consternation of some other nuclear-church leaders.

I can remember that when I taught church growth at Fuller Seminary in the School of World Mission (now the School of

Intercultural Studies), I regularly kindled some strong disapproval of both my ideas and my actions by many of the theologians in the School of Theology because of my pragmatism. Let me give you a concrete example.

Author and pastor John MacArthur and I have known each other for many years. While our paths don't cross often, we keep in touch once in a while, and we have an underlying respect for each other despite some prominent differences. One of these differences is directly related to my pragmatism. In fact, MacArthur features me (as well as others, such as George Barna and Elmer Towns and Doug Murren) in a book, *Ashamed of the Gospel.* He contrasts us with Paul, who wrote, "I am not ashamed of the gospel" (Rom. 1:16). MacArthur writes, "Unfortunately 'ashamed of the gospel' seems more and more apt as a description of some of the most visible and influential churches of our age."[1]

The subtitle of MacArthur's book is very apropos to our attempt to distinguish the nuclear-church rule book from the extended-church rule book. The subtitle is *When the Church Becomes Like the World.* In our terminology, this reflects a concern that the nuclear church might open itself to undue influence by the extended church. Presumably, the church is good, while the world is bad. As I explained in chapter 1, this point of view emerges from the Greek mind-set rather than the Hebrew mind-set, which is more foundational to the church in the workplace. Pragmatism is seen by the typical nuclear-church leader as worldly.

I have carefully read all that John MacArthur says about me and my pragmatism. Everything he says is true! Accusing me of being pragmatic is like accusing the Pope of being Catholic! Here are some of the points that he makes:

> The church has imbibed the worldly philosophy of pragmatism, and we're just beginning to taste the bitter results.[2]

> An overpowering surge of ardent pragmatism is sweeping through evangelicalism.[3]

Perhaps the most visible signs of pragmatism are seen in the convulsive changes that have revolutionized the church worship service in the past decade. Some of evangelicalism's largest and most influential churches now boast Sunday services that are designed purposely to be more rollicking than reverent.[4]

Pragmatism as a philosophy of ministry has gained impetus from the church growth movement that has flourished over the past fifty years or so. Donald McGavran, the father of the modern church growth movement, was an unabashed pragmatist.[5]

C. Peter Wagner, professor of church growth at the Fuller School of World Mission, is Donald McGavran's best-known student.[6]

Wagner, like most in the church growth movement, claims that the "consecrated pragmatism" he advocates does not allow compromise of doctrine or ethics. . . . "But with this proviso," Wagner continues, "we ought to see clearly that the end *does* justify the means. What else possibly could justify the means? If the method I am using accomplishes the goal I am aiming at, it is for that reason a good method. If, on the other hand, my method is not accomplishing the goal, how can I be justified in continuing to use it?" Is that true? Certainly not.[7]

Efficiency

Admittedly, my pragmatism reflects the extended-church rule book. Laura Nash and Scotty McLennan indicate that most extended-church leaders would agree with me. Pragmatism surfaced as a core issue in their research that lead to *Church on Sunday, Work on Monday*. "Take, for example, the question of efficiency," they write. "Businesspeople place great emphasis on efficiency and its related value of pragmatism. In its extreme free-market form, efficiency is seen as a moral corrective—a way of securing fair prices without governmental tyranny."[8] Their point of view, which comes from the extended-church rule book, sees pragmatism as a moral high road, quite a contrast to the nuclear-church rule book, as we have just seen.

"Such differing attitudes, which reflect deep moral viewpoints, are a significant feature of the distanced relationship," Nash and McLennan explain, before citing a fascinating illustration of this "distanced relationship" between the nuclear church and the extended church in the area of pragmatism.[9] They tell the story of a CEO of a $100 million company who decided to retire and enroll in seminary for the purpose of personal enrichment. "The transition was difficult," they write.

> By his own admission, the theological community perceived him as too outspoken, too impatient, and too superficially pragmatic. He seethed over the memory of registering for classes: "I don't understand inefficiency. It's an insult to people. We had to stand in line for three hours to register. Three hours! They knew how many people would attend, and yet there was no mechanism to register more quickly."[10]

That statement, coming from the point of view of the extended-church rule book, would offend many nuclear-church leaders. Nash and McLennan found the following to be true:

> Many pastors and seminarians we interviewed felt that efficiency in operations was not a priority; in their view it represented ruthlessness and insensitivity to people's emotional needs. Clergy mistrusted pragmatism. It played into their caricature of the shallowness and hard-heartedness of businesspeople.[11]

The Nuclear-Church Rule Book

I have had my share of experiences with the nuclear-church rule book. Years ago, for example, I agreed to serve as a member of a committee in my Congregational church. Our purpose was to help guide the church through an important decision for the future. The months went by with subcommittees and study commissions and time-consuming weekly meetings that seemed endless as we went around in circles. Finally, after six months, the chairperson of the committee suggested that we go back to the congregation with "A Plan for Planning"! I respectfully asked to step down from the committee.

At about the same time, I was serving on the faculty of a theological seminary that was also making an important decision. I lost count of the number of joint faculty meetings and study reports that related to the issues at stake. Finally, when everyone seemed to be at the point of exhaustion, the president, in a gesture of encouragement, said, "After all, the process is much more important than the final outcome"! I was so stunned that I have never forgotten those words.

When things like that happen, nuclear-church leaders have been trained to say, "We must always be thankful that God has not called us to be successful; He has only called us to be faithful!" I, pragmatic Peter, wilt inside whenever I hear that statement. I could not imagine a workplace apostle saying something so ridiculous.

Investing the Talents

One thing I wonder when nuclear-church leaders say that it doesn't matter whether they are successful as long as they are faithful is whether they have ever read the parable of the talents, a parable that is focused directly on the workplace (see Matt. 25:14-30). Jesus tells the parable of a capitalist (an entrepreneur, a businessman) who calls in three of his employees. The man gives to one employee five talents (let's say that is $50,000), to another two ($20,000) and to another one ($10,000). He sends them out to do their thing, which is not even defined in the parable because it is assumed that everyone knows that he gives them money so that they will make more money.

The employee given $50,000 comes back with $100,000. The master says to him, "Well done, good and faithful servant" (Matt. 25:21). Note that he called the man faithful. The master says the same thing to the employee given $20,000, who brings back $40,000. Why were both of these employees *faithful*? Because they were *successful* in using the master's resources for the master's purpose. But when the employee who received $10,000 brings back the same $10,000, the master calls him a "wicked and lazy servant" (v. 26), and he fired him on the spot!

The parable of the talents *unites* success and faithfulness. It is a Hebrew parable, and pragmatism was not anathema to the Hebrews. Those who try to separate success and faithfulness are captives of the Greek mind-set.

Another equally common nuclear-church (Greek) concept is, "It doesn't matter what I *do*; it only matters who I *am.*" The thought behind this is, *"Being* is much more important than *doing;* who I *am* is more important than what I *do.*" For the extended-church rule book, such a statement is pure nonsense. How can I possibly separate what I am from what I do? That is why Jesus said, "By their fruits you will know them" (Matt. 7:20).

In terms of the means and the end, the differences between the nuclear-church rule book and the extended-church rule book are clear. Which rule book to you prefer?

Rule 8

Tough **Calls**

A basic premise of this book is that each of the two forms of the church, the nuclear church and the extended church, has its own culture and its own rule book. Moving between the two cultures is a way of life for workplace believers. However, most pastors and other nuclear-church leaders spend virtually all of their time in just one culture. In light of this, it would be correct to say that traditional church leaders have a monocultural perspective, while workplace people have a cross-cultural perspective.

Written and Unwritten Laws

Those of us who have been field missionaries have, by necessity, learned to operate out of different cultural rule books. It wasn't easy for Doris and me because we grew up in the America of the Great Depression and World War II, which valued honesty, integrity, discipline, loyalty, faithfulness and reverence. We learned one of our first lessons when we tried to get the few possessions that we took to the field with us through customs. Like America, Bolivia had written laws about importing foreign goods. Unlike America, however, Bolivia had unwritten laws that allowed customs officials, first, to interpret the written laws as they wished and, second, to add fees that were not prescribed by law for their personal services. This modus operandi was not a secret, like some Enron scandal; it was the normal way of doing business in that culture.

Not only had Doris and I come from America, but also we had just studied Christian ethics in Bible school and seminary. We were taught that offering a bribe to a government official was a sin.

Consequently, we were faced with one of our first cross-cultural tough calls. What should we do? Refuse to pay the supplementary fees (were they bribes?) and, in all probability, never see our belongings (which included our wedding pictures)?

We were wise enough to ask advice from our senior missionary colleagues, who had long since become bicultural. They were quite comfortable with both rule books. They advised us to hire a lawyer who specialized in customs affairs and to pay his fee, but to not ask him for receipts to show how he spent the money we had given him. We did so, and we soon had our belongings. Everyone was happy, including the customs official who was applying the unwritten law of the nation.

A Friend in the Police Station

Then we needed driver's licenses. We were told that the best way to get a driver's license was to have a friend in the police station. At that time, one could easily make friends with someone in the police station for about 30 pesos. We proceeded to make a friend who then provided us with some inside information. Even though we turned out to be some of the few missionaries I knew of who actually had to take some tests, we soon had our driver's licenses. On the other hand, I recall a Methodist missionary who, at about the same time, had just come to Bolivia in order to clean up corruption in the nation. He looked up the written law and declared that he was going to get his driver's license in the legal way. After six months of struggling, he decided that he would also make a friend in the police station!

When we came back to America, we did not tell these stories in churches. By that time we were functioning comfortably under both cultural rule books, but we knew that those who had been operating under only one rule book would have a hard time understanding the tough calls that we constantly had to make on the mission field.

This cross-cultural dilemma applies equally to workplace believers. Perhaps not all, but certainly a large number of them, make tough calls during the week that they know their pastor would not understand, so they simply don't talk about them. What is going through their minds? *My pastor doesn't have a clue about what life is like out there in the real world!*

Give Business Some Ethics!

The fact that this cultural gap exists has been confirmed sociologically by Laura Nash and Scotty McLennan. They asked nuclear-church leaders, "What, if anything, would you change in the way the church deals with business issues and business thinking?" By far, the answer they heard most frequently was, "change the way businesspeople think," or some variation thereof.[1] Later they asked clergy, "What would you do to change business attitudes in relation to faith?" One of the most common answers was, "Give it some ethics."[2] Notice what thought these responses imply: *My nuclear-church rule book is better than your extended-church rule book in the area of ethics. I have ethics, and you don't.*

Where are pastors getting such ideas from? Nash and McLennan have spent some time probing this question, and they have perceptively identified a number of "fundamental differences of direction and power that express their deeply divergent worldviews."[3] What are those differences? Nash and McLennan explain:

> Business people tend to favor an additive approach, ecclesiastics a subtractive one. For example, when asked about solutions for economic injustice, the church frequently suggests giving away possessions and earnings, while businesspeople suggest creating more jobs. . . . The ecclesiastic tends to interpret along a path of self-denial (subtraction), the businessperson along a path of self-interest.[4]

Not only does this highlight important differences between the two rule books, but it also reflects some of the entrenchment that the spirit of poverty has attained in churches across the board.

Ethical decision making permeates the atmosphere of the extended church. Believers out in the workplace must make tough calls. Nuclear-church leaders tend to look at ethical decisions in terms of right or wrong, white or black. "True," nuclear-church leaders might say, "there may be some areas of gray, but these are exceptions to the rule; and the gray areas, when they come up, are narrow." Pastors will teach their businesspeople this guiding, ethical principle: "Make the *right* decision, not the *easy* one." They commonly teach that if you live by the Golden Rule, you will know right from wrong.

Life Is Complex

However, ethics in the workplace are not always that simple. For example, Linda Rios Brook says:

> Life is much more complex than making a good decision or making a bad decision. Sometimes you do not have an option between a good decision and a bad decision. The only option is between a bad decision and a worse decision. That's much harder because you don't have fans, only critics, on both sides of the argument.[5]

Linda was facing a situation like this when she was president and general manager of KLGT-TV, Channel 23, in Minneapolis/St. Paul (which, incidentally, she purchased at a closeout sale for $3 million and sold seven years later for $52.5 million net to the shareholders). At one point, she decided to purchase the Rush Limbaugh Show for her audience. However, it turned out that the syndication house that owned the Rush Limbaugh Show also owned the Jerry Springer Show, and they wouldn't let Linda have the one without the other. This became a tough call. She decidedly did not want KLGT to be associated with Jerry Springer in the public mind. Nevertheless, in order to get Rush Limbaugh, she took Jerry Springer as well.

Did Linda receive criticism from the nuclear church? In her book *Frontline Christians in a Bottom-Line World*, Linda tells, "I hated the fact that many of my Christian colleagues were outraged I had made such a compromise."[6]

The next decision that Linda made was to put the Jerry Springer Show on so late at night that hardly anyone would watch it. But much to her surprise, it became her highest-rated show and the most profitable one. What to do now? Linda is a woman of prayer, and it was in a prayer meeting that God showed Linda that those who watched Jerry Springer at midnight were "people who were looking for someone whose circumstances were worse than their own." As Linda explains, "Sometimes the only way we feel better is to find someone who feels worse."[7]

Evangelism with Jerry Springer

Now that she had this in mind, Brook was prepared to receive an unexpected vision from God. She saw Jerry Springer on a television monitor with lines of words coming across the bottom like a severe weather alert. The words were "Need a friend? Call 555-5555," which happened to be the number of a Christian counseling center run by friends of hers. Her friends agreed to let her do it. The results? Here's how Linda tells it:

> The volume of calls that flooded into the crisis center that night shut their telephone system down. For more than four years, extra counselors had to be on duty from midnight to 3:00 a.m. to handle the calls from people who were so desperate and lost, they would reach out for a friend anywhere they could find one. Thousands of people were led to Jesus during those years.[8]

Operating from the extended-church rule book, Linda Rios Brook was elated that God could use Jerry Springer as a platform for evangelism. But now comes the sad part: "Even though this story became quite well-known in the Midwest, I never received a single positive phone call from any of my many clergy friends," she tells.[9] Apparently, Linda had bent the rules of the nuclear church's rule book a bit too far.

What did the nuclear-church leaders want? Brook explains, "Many voiced that I should have tried to get the Billy Graham Crusades on my channel. I would have gladly done that very thing if it had been an option, but it was not. I did not have a choice between good and bad or good and better. My choice was between bad and worse."[10]

Linda's disillusionment with the nuclear-church rule book comes across in this thoughtful statement:

> Many times there is no acceptable compromise for the king [the workplace leader] to make. But, sometimes there is; and if and when this is the case, the king should be supported as he or she tries to find a way through a jungle where competitors shoot with real guns. Sad to say, but in my experience those who advise the kings to leave the kingdom rather than find a compromise of any kind are those who don't have a kingdom to lose.[11]

Where to Draw the Line

Workplace believers are called upon to make the tough calls, to choose between bad and worse, to compromise when necessary. However, all workplace believers agree that there are ethical, moral and spiritual lines you do not cross. Both Daniel and Joseph rose to the top because they were able to adapt cross-culturally to the Babylonian and Egyptian cultures in which they found themselves. For both of them, their careers involved many tough calls. However, Daniel would not compromise at the line of idolatry, and Joseph would not compromise at the line of immorality.

Likewise, Paul Gazelka found himself in a potentially compromising situation in Paris soon after he was awarded a major promotion to manager in his company. While there, Paul and his wife were invited to a very important business dinner at the Moulin Rouge, a prestigious restaurant known to entertain its clients with topless dancing. Paul asks rhetorically, "What was I to do? I wanted the opportunity to meet this group of agents, but I certainly did not want to promote that kind of entertainment."[12]

Paul called the restaurant and thought he understood through the broken English conversation that the dancing began after dessert. He and his wife decided to go and to just slip out unobtrusively after dessert before the entertainment started, with no embarrassment to anyone. Paul had misunderstood, however, and the dancing actually came with the dessert. Another tough call. What did he do? "We were in a very tight spot with little room for a gracious exit," Paul explains. "We looked at each other, got up, and simply said we had to leave. It was obvious to the group why we were leaving. We really didn't say anything, but they knew. Without having to say anything, we had set a new standard for our leadership style."[13]

Moving into the Workplace

Now that the Body of Christ is beginning to understand ministry in the workplace, workplace apostles and our mandate to take dominion and transform society, God is beginning to lead high-profile nuclear-church apostles into assuming significant roles in the extended church. This is a high-risk transition, and it involves many tough calls.

For example, Keith Butler, a prominent apostle and pastor of the 21,000-member Word of Faith International Christian Center in Detroit, felt the call of God to run for the United States Senate. Predictably, many nuclear-church leaders have raised their eyebrows at the thought of a preacher stepping down and becoming a politician.

In Singapore, the pastors of the two largest churches in the city have ventured into the workplace without resigning their pulpits. Both are recognized apostles and are members of the International Coalition of Apostles.

The Magic of Love
Lawrence Khong is one of these pastors. He has shown great interest and superior skill at the art of illusion, or magic, since he was 10 years old. This is not the kind of magic that calls upon supernatural, occult

powers, but rather it is the kind that creates illusions with sleight of hand, smoke and mirrors. Lawrence frequently reminds his audience, "Things are not what they seem."

Lawrence, along with his daughter, Priscilla, has developed a highly professional show that uses the magic to carry the audience through a modern version of the parable of the prodigal son. This show, "The Magic of Love," has become popular throughout Southeast Asia and China. Lawrence has performed in America and has received excellent reviews. It is not performed in churches, but in secular theaters, where he honors God in his concluding statements and, with his team, ministers personally to people after the show.

Lawrence has received a good bit of criticism from nuclear-church leaders. In fact, a substantial segment of his congregation left when he began this new ministry in the workplace (he has since gained an equal number back). Khong's desire, among other things, is to become a literal celebrity in China so that he can have a voice that no Christian pastor per se could have in order to help transform society there. He is a nuclear-church leader following the extended-church rule book.

A Pop-Music Minister

Kong Hee and his wife, Sun Ho, are the founding leaders of City Harvest Church, the largest church in Singapore. The church has grown and continues to grow at a rapid rate. In 2002, Sun Ho, a musician and the worship leader at the church, felt that the Lord was calling her to move into the marketplace by entering the pop-music field. She began slowly, never imagining that she would go to the top of her field in two or three years. At this writing, she is the most popular singer in China, a legitimate celebrity (she sings in Mandarin and in English). Her name is a household word through all of Southeast Asia. She has topped the charts twice in the United States and twice in the United Kingdom, the first Asian to do either.

With the tremendous amount of income that this new workplace ministry generates, Sun Ho has established humanitarian foundations. Her relief team was the first one to reach Banda Aceh,

Indonesia, after the 2004 tsunami hit. In the first three days, her team's surgeon, Dr. Francis Seow-Choen, performed almost 50 operations. Sun Ho wants to build a modern school building in each of China's 13 largest cities; two are already completed. The Chinese government admires Sun Ho so much that it has issued a commemorative postage stamp honoring her. She has been on the cover of several magazines. And she still pastors and leads worship as a volunteer at City Harvest.

Like Lawrence Khong, Sun Ho and her husband, Kong Hee, have received severe criticism from some nuclear-church leaders. One tough call that Sun Ho had to make was modeling a dress from an international fashion designer while she was in Hollywood. When some pastors in Singapore saw her picture, they thought that the dress was too scanty, so they convened a special public event to share their outrage with each other and to oppose the idea of a Christian leader's singing pop music. The good news is that City Harvest Church fully backs her new ministry.

Apostolic leaders like Keith Butler, Lawrence Kong and Sun Ho are writing some new pages in the extended-church rule book. They know how to make tough calls.

Conclusion

As I conclude this section on the two rule books, I feel both good and not so good. I feel good because, to my knowledge, no one has previously attempted to systematically enumerate the contrasts between the nuclear-church rule book and the extended-church rule book. The eight rules that I have been able to flesh out are an excellent beginning to a process that will undoubtedly be ongoing for some time to come.

I feel not so good because I know that there are many more than eight rules and I wish that I could have completed the list. In this conclusion, however, I would like to simply suggest four other areas in which I think there are significant differences between the two cultures. Perhaps someone else can elaborate on them one of these days.

Alliances

Under extended-church rules, part of normal life consists of making alliances of one kind or another with those who may or may not have the same belief system or who may or may not adhere to the same moral code, but who can add value to you and to whom you can also add value. For example, Daniel agreed to supervise the Babylonian government office, which employed magicians, astrologers and soothsayers (see Dan. 5:11). Likewise, a Christian who has holdings in the Middle East might conceivable find it convenient to establish a business partnership with a Muslim.

The nuclear-church rules, on the other hand, take a considerably more cautious approach. The starting point for many of the clergy is 2 Corinthians 6:14-15: "Do not be unequally yoked together with unbelievers. For what fellowship has righteousness with lawlessness? And what communion has light with darkness? And what accord has Christ with Belial? Or what part has a believer with an unbeliever?"

In some areas, such as political structures, school systems, the military and most occupations, these verses are not applied literally. On the other hand, pastors typically consider the guideline normative for marriage or close friendships or business partnerships. Should a Christian businessperson go into partnership or otherwise associate closely with an unbeliever? The nuclear church's implied answer to this question is no. The ethical standards of the businessperson who enters into partnership with a Muslim, for example, would be regarded as unbiblical.

Doctrine

Those of us who have studied in traditional Bible schools and seminaries know that the conventional wisdom among those who develop the curriculum for training nuclear-church leaders is that studying and mastering doctrine are essential. By reviewing the course of study for my Master of Divinity degree, for example, I have calculated that my courses related to doctrine would have cost me $10,000 at today's prices. Doctrine obviously has a high value in the nuclear-church rule book.

Placing high value on doctrine does not carry over to the extended-church rule book. Most nuclear-church leaders, if they were flying somewhere, would tend to check two large suitcases of doctrine. Extended-church leaders, on the other hand, would probably make the same trip with a small carry-on.

By saying this, I do not mean to denigrate the importance of doctrine, particularly the standard, evangelical set of what all would agree are absolute doctrinal principles, such as the sovereignty of God, the authority of Scripture, the deity of Christ, justification by faith, the ministry of the Holy Spirit, the priesthood of all believers, the second coming of Christ, and the power of prayer (this is not an exhaustive list). These are doctrines of both rule books.

One of the reasons that nuclear-church leaders consider doctrinal details important is because, by and large, they were trained by professional theologians and scholars. The party line is that solid doctrine is necessary for Christian maturity; it helps draw the lines to differentiate your church or denomination from others; it is a test of accurate Bible knowledge; and it is a badge of closeness to God.

When I was in seminary, I was required to pass tests on the filoque clause, anthropomorphism, predestination, Pelagianism, supralapsarianism and infralapsarianism, substitutionary atonement, homousios versus homoiusios, and much more. When I got into the real world, however, I was surprised that there were believers who had excellent Christian character and whose ministry surpassed mine in many areas but who had never passed a test on any of the above.

Most believers in the extended church are not overly concerned about whether the church is to be raptured before the tribulation or whether babies should be baptized or whether tongues is the initial physical evidence of baptism in the Holy Spirit or whether Holy Communion is a sacrament or whether God has foreknowledge of every decision that we make. They tend to be doctrinal minimalists, paying little attention to the fact that every one of the doctrinal items that I just mentioned has been and still is a subject of energetic debate among nuclear-church leaders.

Spiritual Authority

Up until recently, most nuclear-church leaders assumed that all spiritual authority is to be traced up through the nuclear church. What that means is that all workplace believers are required to join a local church and that all place themselves under the spiritual authority of the pastor of that church. This nuclear-church rule has become such common currency that I suppose if George Barna were to take a poll, he would find that a huge percentage of believers still agree with it. The fact of the matter is that this rule was developed in the days, not too long ago, when hardly anyone was aware that there was even such a thing as a church in the workplace.

Once we begin to admit that there might be such a thing as a church in the workplace, another question arises: Is the church in the workplace just as legitimate a form of the church as the traditional nuclear church, or is it slightly inferior? I have talked to nuclear-church leaders who feel that the extended church is essentially a derivative of the nuclear church and who consequently assume a position of final spiritual authority.

Many workplace leaders today would question that thinking. For one thing, as the church in the workplace takes form, it is typically made up of believers who belong to a wide variety of local churches and denominations. One of the reasons that these diverse believers can come together in meaningful and productive relationships is that, by and large, they are doctrinal minimalists. On Sundays, their church's doctrinal distinctives are important, but Monday through Saturday, doctrine decidedly takes a back seat to other considerations.

Workplace believers will especially be able to come together in meaningful relationships when extended-church apostles, prophets, evangelists, pastors and teachers are set in place and properly recognized. Tensions are bound to arise when believers find themselves under the spiritual authority of two pastors: a nuclear-church pastor and a workplace pastor. And the tensions will certainly increase as extended-church apostles move into the fullness of their ministry, serving as spiritual peers to nuclear-church apostles.

Such tensions can be greatly reduced or even neutralized if leaders across the board recognize, understand and affirm the validity of each other's spiritual authority and rule book.

Accountability

Guidelines for accountability are fairly well-established in the Body of Christ. To most believers, there will not be much of a discernable difference between the nuclear-church rule book and the extended-church rule book. But to some, there will be noticeable differences, particularly to those in higher positions of leadership.

As I have been testing these waters, two internationally respected businesspeople have said virtually the same thing to me:

Peter, I am committed to my church both personally and financially. I admire and respect my pastor, and I enjoy the Sunday services. Having said that, as a businessperson I desperately need serious intercession for the business transactions I am making on a regular basis. However, I could never tell my pastor about them, nor would I entrust the information to any of the prayer groups in my church.

An obvious implication of a statement like this is that these businesspeople do not feel a sense of accountability to their local church for the operation of their businesses. They undoubtedly feel local-church accountability for their ministry to their families or for their personal lifestyle or for their spiritual disciplines or for their moral behavior. However, at the same time, they know that their pastor has few insights on company finances or business ethics or managing personnel or venture capital or import-export complexities, the very things for which they need prayer and spiritual guidance to handle properly.

I raise this extremely important question because I'm not sure that the extended church as yet has clear enough guidelines for answering it. Undoubtedly, when workplace apostles become more prominent, they will be able to set this is order. Meanwhile, others are seeking solutions. John Beehner of Jacksonville, Florida, for example, has established a ministry called Wise Counsel, which brings together groups of up to 12 peer-level businesspeople. High commitment to the group is required and validated by substantial membership fees and expected attendance at monthly gatherings. Among other things, Wise Counsel members hold themselves accountable to each other.

Financial counselor Larry Burkett suggests this:

Set up an accountability group. A businessperson can also set up an impartial group of Christian advisers. I know that it may be difficult in many areas of the country to find Christians who will agree to serve in this capacity. An alternative is to link up with one or two others in similar businesses in other parts of the country and communicate on major decisions by phone, fax, or email.[1]

This crucial issue of workplace accountability will remain high on the agenda of those of us who continue the quest to bring substance and clarification to the differences between the nuclear-church rule book and the extended-church rule book. It will be an ongoing process for several years to come, and new issues will certainly surface on a regular basis.

I find it impossible to write a concluding paragraph to this book because I believe that we have just begun and that our work is a work in progress. I can, however, pray for the mighty hand of God to move through His people in such a way that together the nuclear church and the extended church will see very soon the literal transformation of our society with God's kingdom manifesting on the earth as it is in heaven!

Endnotes

Chapter 1

1. Throughout this book I am using the term "marketplace" as a synonym to "workplace," even though later in the book I explain that I prefer the term "workplace."
2. Myles Monroe, "Apostolic Moments," *The Voice* (April 2005), p. 40.
3. Jack Graham (lecture, Second Baptist Church, Houston, TX, n.d.).
4. John Beckett, *Loving Monday* (Downers Grove, IL: InterVarsity Press, 1998), p. 67.
5. Ibid.
6. Dennis Peacocke, "Co-Managing the Earth," *Business Reform*, vol. 3, no. 6, p. 60.
7. James Thwaites, *Renegotiating the Church Contract* (Carlisle, England: Paternoster Press, 2001), pp. 30-31.
8. David Oliver and James Thwaites, *Church That Works* (Milton Keynes, England: Word Publishing, 2001), p. 58.
9. Robert J. Tamasy, ed. *Jesus Works Here* (Nashville, TN: Broadman and Holman Publishers, 1995), p. 3.
10. Mark Greene, *Thank GOD It's Monday: Ministry in the Workplace* (Bletchley, England: Scripture Union, 2001), p. 104.
11. Gregory F. A. Pierce, *spirituality@work* (Chicago: Loyola Press, 2001), p. 19.

Chapter 2

1. For details on the New Apostolic Reformation, see my book *Churchquake!* (Ventura, CA: Regal Books, 1999). For specific statistics, see David B. Barrett and Todd M. Johnson, "Annual Statistical Table of Global Mission," *International Bulletin of Missionary Research* (January 2003), p. 25; David B. Barrett and Todd M. Johnson, *World Christian Trends, AD 30-AD 2200* (Pasadena, CA: William Carey Library, 2001), p. 302. Barrett's terms "Independent," "Postdenominational" and "Neo-Apostolic" refer to the same global phenomenon to which "New Apostolic Reformation" refers.
2. For details on the Second Apostolic Age, see my book *Changing Church* (Ventura, CA: Regal Books, 2004).
3. Megan Doyle, "Relationship Between the Church and Business Community," in Rich Marshall, *God@Work* (Shippensburg, PA: Destiny Image, 2000), p. 107.
4. Stephanie Klinzing, quoted in Ed Silvoso, *God's Ticker Tape* (San Jose, CA: Harvest Evangelism, 2003), p. 67.
5. Rich Marshall, *God@Work, Volume 2* (Shippensburg, PA: Destiny Image, 2005), p. 7.

Chapter 3

1. Bill Hamon, e-mail to Christian International Ministries Network mailing list, May 19, 2005.
2. Wesley Duewel, *Revival Fire* (Grand Rapids, MI: Zondervan Publishing House, 1995), p. 46.
3. Eddie Long, *Taking Over* (Lake Mary, FL: Charisma House, 1999), p. 6.
4. Mario Roberto Morales, "La Quiebra de Maximón," *Crónica Semanal* (June 24-30, 1994), p. 94. My translation.
5. Long, *Taking Over*, p. 134.
6. Jack Hayford, "Pastor's Heart," *Ministries Today* (July-August 2004), p. 72.

Chapter 4

1. Joe Johnson, "The Opening Bell," *Business Reform* (January/February 2002), p. 3. Emphasis in original.
2. Ibid.
3. Ibid.
4. Ibid.
5. Barbara Wentroble, "God Is Doing Something New," *IbM Newsletter* (January 2005), p. 1.
6. Laura Nash and Scotty McLennan, *Church on Sunday, Work on Monday* (San Francisco: Jossey-Bass, 2001), p. 128.
7. Ibid., p. 129.
8. Joel Osteen, *Your Best Life Now* (New York: Warner Faith, 2004), pp. 85-86.
9. Ibid.
10. Richard Fleming, *The Glory Returns to the Workplace* (San Giovanni Teatino, Italy: Destiny Image Europe, 2004), p. 9.
11. Ibid.
12. Larry Hutch, *Free at Last* (New Kensington, PA: Whitaker House, 2004), p. 132.
13. Ibid.
14. Chuck D. Pierce and Robert Heidler, *Restoring Your Shield of Faith* (Ventura, CA: Regal Books, 2004), p. 23.
15. John Dawson, *Taking Our Cities for God* (Lake Mary, FL: Creation House, 1989), p. 193.
16. Ibid.
17. Charles Edward White, "What Wesley Practiced and Preached about Money," *Mission Frontiers,* 1994. http://www.missionfrontiers.org/archive.htm (accessed November 7, 2005).

Chapter 5

1. Rick Kirkland, "Faith and Fortune," *Fortune* (July 9, 2001), p. 18.
2. Ibid.
3. Marc Gunther, quoted in Kirkland, "Faith and Fortune," p. 18.
4. Ibid.
5. Marc Gunther, "God and Business," *Fortune* (July 9, 2001), p. 61.
6. Ibid.
7. Ibid., p. 64.
8. Ted DeMoss and Robert Tamasy, *The Gospel and the Briefcase* (Chattanooga, TN: CBMC Publications, 1984), p. 51.
9. Robert J. Tamasy, ed., *Jesus Works Here* (Nashville, TN: Broadman and Holman Publishers, 1995), p. 254.
10. J.R. Zeigler, "Full Gospel Business Men's Fellowship International," *The New International Dictionary of Pentecostal and Charismatic Movements,* ed. Stanley M. Burgess (Grand Rapids, MI: Zondervan Publishing House, 2002), p. 653.
11. DeMoss and Tamasy, *The Gospel and the Briefcase,* p. 83.
12. Zeigler, "Full Gospel Business Men's Fellowship International," p. 653.
13. Os Hillman, *Faith@Work* (Cumming, GA: Aslan Group Publishing, 2004), p. 2.
14. Ibid., p. 5.
15. Ibid.
16. Os Hillman, e-mail to author, updating the information in *Faith@Work,* n.d.

17. Ralph Cochran, "From the Director's Desk," *Business Reform*, vol. 3, no. 1 (2002), p. 5.

18. Rich Marshall, *God@Work* (Shippensburg, PA: Destiny Image Publishers, 2000), p. 5.

19. Russell Shorto, "Faith at Work," *The New York Times Magazine* (October 31, 2004), p. 42.

20. Ibid.

21. Ibid., p. 43.

22. Ibid.

Chapter 6

1. Richelle Wiseman, "Linking Sunday with Monday," *Faith Today* (January/February 2003), p. 24.

2. Ibid.

3. Peter Tsukahira, *My Father's Business* (Haifa, Israel: privately published, 2000), p. 19.

4. Paul Gazelka, *Marketplace Ministers* (Lake Mary, FL: Creation House Press, 2003), p. 70.

5. Laura Nash and Scotty McLennan, *Church on Sunday, Work on Monday* (San Francisco: Jossey-Bass, 2001), p. 9.

6. Ibid., p. xxvi.

7. Ibid., p. 124.

8. Ibid., p. 10.

9. Ibid., p. 129.

10. Paul Anderson and Graeme Sellers, "The Myth of the Lay Person, *ARC,* p. 1. http://arcusa.org/dw_articles/TheMythoftheLayPerson.pdf (accessed November 5, 2005).

11. Ibid.

12. Ibid., pp. 1,4.

13. Ibid., p. 6.

Introduction to the Rule Books

1. Laura Nash and Scotty McLennan, *Church on Sunday, Work on Monday* (San Francisco: Jossey-Bass, 2001), p. 128.

2. Peter Tsukahira, *My Father's Business* (Haifa, Israel: privately published, 2000), p. 67.

Rule 1

1. Kent and Davidene Humphreys, *Show and Then Tell* (Chicago: Moody Press, 2000), pp. 21-22.

2. Robert E. Fraser, *Marketplace Christianity* (Overland Park, KS: New Grid Publishing, 2004), p. 56.

3. Quoted in Laura Nash, *Believers in Business* (Nashville, TN: Thomas Nelson, 1994), p. 60.

4. C. Peter Wagner, *Your Spiritual Gifts Can Help Your Church Grow,* rev. ed. (Ventura, CA: Regal Books, 2005), p. 33.

5. Jack W. MacGorman, *The Gifts of the Spirit* (Nashville, TN: Broadman Press, 1974), p. 31.

6. Wagner, *Your Spiritual Gifts*, 1994 ed., p. 35.

7. Ed Silvoso, *Anointed for Business* (Ventura, CA: Regal Books, 2002), p. 34.

8. Ibid.

9. Nash, *Believers in Business,* p. 64.

Rule 2

1. Bill Hamon, *The Day of the Saints* (Shippensburg, PA: Destiny Image, 2000), p. 251.

2. Ana Méndez, *Sentados en Lugares Celestiales* (privately published, 2002), p. 20. My translation.

3. See Rich Marshall, *God@Work, Volume 2* (Shippensburg, PA: Destiny Image, 2005), p. 7.

4. Hamon, *The Day of the Saints*, pp. 269-270.

5. John Kelly, *End-Time Warriors* (Ventura, CA: Regal Books, 1999), p. 54.

6. See, for example, Ed Silvoso, "Miracle in the Marketplace," *Charisma* (September 2004), p. 49.

7. Hamon, *The Day of the Saints*, pp. 251-252.

8. Loren Cunningham, *Making Jesus Lord* (Seattle, WA: YWAM Publishing, 1988), p. 134.

9. Lance Wallnau, "A Prophetic, Biblical, and Personal Call to the Marketplace," privately circulated paper, nd., np.

10. Ibid.

11. Ibid.

12. Ibid.

13. Linda Rios Brook, *Frontline Christians in a Bottom-Line World* (Shippensburg, PA: Destiny Image, 2004), p. 176.

14. Ibid.

15. Ibid.

16. Ibid.

17. Ibid.

Rule 3

1. Peter Tsukahira, *My Father's Business* (Haifa, Israel: privately published, 2000), p. 86.

2. Laura Nash and Scotty McLennan, *Church on Sunday, Work on Monday* (San Francisco: Jossey-Bass, 2001), p. 173.

3. Megan Doyle, unpublished address to Dallas prayer leaders, August 1, 2001, p. 3.

4. Ed Silvoso, *Anointed for Business* (Ventura, CA: Regal Books, 2002), pp. 73-74.

5. The National Shrine of Saint Francis of Assisi, "Francis Discerns His Vocation More Fully," 2002. http://www.shrinesf.org/francis02.htm (accessed November 7, 2005).

6. Charles Edward White, "What Wesley Practiced and Preached about Money," *Mission Frontiers,* 1994. http://www.missionfrontiers.org/archive.htm (accessed November 7, 2005).

7. Rich Marshall, *God@Work, Volume 2* (Shippensburg, PA: Destiny Image, 2005), pp. 66-67.

8. Ibid., p. 70.

Rule 4

1. David R. High, *Kings and Priests* (Oklahoma City, OK: Books for the Children of the World, 1993), p. 4.

2. Ibid., p. 5.

3. Peter Lyne, *First Apostles, Last Apostles* (Tonbridge, England: Sovereign World, 1999), p. 111.

4. Gregory F. A. Pierce, *spirituality@work* (Chicago: Loyola Press, 2001), p. 119.

5. Lyne, *First Apostles, Last Apostles*, p. 110.

6. David Oliver, *Work: Prison or Place of Destiny?* (Milton Keynes, England: Word Publishing, 1999), p. 103.

7. Ibid.

8. Pierce, *spirituality@work*, p. 121.

Rule 5

1. Mark Greene, *Supporting Christians at Work* (Sheffield, England: Administry, 2001), p. 10.
2. Ibid.
3. Ibid.
4. George Barna, *Revolution* (Wheaton, IL: Tyndale House Publishers, 2005), p. 33.
5. Bill Hybles, *Christians in the Marketplace* (Wheaton, IL: Victor Books, 1982), p. 90.
6. Ralph Moore and Alan Tang, *Your Money* (Ventura, CA: Regal Books, 2004), p. 55.
7. Wolfgang Simson, *Houses That Change the World* (Carlisle, England: Paternoster Publishing, 1998), p. 125.

Rule 6

1. George Barna, *Revolution* (Wheaton, IL: Tyndale House Publishers, 2005), p. 134.
2. Ibid., p. 135.
3. Andy Butcher, "When Christians Quit Church," *Charisma* (February 2005), p. 34.
4. "Letters," *Charisma* (April 2005), p. 8.
5. Ibid.
6. Ibid.
7. Ibid., pp. 8,10.
8. Ibid., p. 10.
9. Ibid.
10. George Barna, *Grow Your Church from the Outside In* (Ventura, CA: Regal Books, 2005), p. 26.
11. Ibid., p. 81.
12. The Barna Group, "Twentysomethings Struggle to Find Their Place in Christian Churches," *The Barna Update,* September 24, 2003. http://www.barna.org/FlexPage .aspx?Page=BarnaUpdate&BarnaUpdateID=149 (accessed November 7, 2005).
13. Barna, *Revolution,* p. 49.
14. Linda Rios Brook, "Marketplace Apostles," privately circulated paper, 2001, p. 2.
15. *Phoenix,* translated by David Wang in "Third Church Making Better Chinese," *Asian Report* (March/April 2005), p. 1.
16. Larry Kreider, *House Church Networks* (Ephrata, PA: House to House Publications, 2001), p. 1.
17. Ibid.
18. Linda Rios Brook, *Frontline Christians in a Bottom-Line World* (Shippensburg, PA: Destiny Image, 2004), p. 22.
19. Sergio Scataglini, quoted in Julian Lukins, "The Virtual Church," *Charisma* (June 2005), p. 67.

Rule 7

1. John F. MacArthur, *Ashamed of the Gospel* (Wheaton, IL: Crossway Books, 1993), p. xix.
2. Ibid.
3. Ibid., p. xiii.
4. Ibid.
5. Ibid., p. 74.
6. Ibid., p. 75.
7. Ibid., pp. 75-76.
8. Laura Nash and Scotty McLennan, *Church on Sunday, Work on Monday* (San Francisco: Jossey-Bass, 2001), p. 139.

9. Ibid., p. 140.

10. Ibid.

11. Ibid.

Rule 8

1. Laura Nash and Scotty McLennan, *Church on Sunday, Work on Monday* (San Francisco: Jossey-Bass, 2001), p. 126.

2. Ibid., p. 130.

3. Ibid., p. 197.

4. Ibid.

5. Linda Rios Brook, quoted in Larry S. Julian, *God Is My CEO* (Holbrook, MA: Adams Media Corporation, 2001.), p. 139.

6. Linda Rios Brook, *Frontline Christians in a Bottom-Line World* (Shippensburg, PA: Destiny Image, 2004), p. 133.

7. Ibid.

8. Ibid., p. 134.

9. Ibid.

10. Ibid.

11. Ibid., pp. 134-135.

12. Paul Gazelka, *Marketplace Ministers* (Lake Mary, FL: Creation House Press, 2003), p. 16.

13. Ibid., p. 17.

Conclusion

1. Larry Burkett, *Business by the Book* (Nashville, TN: Thomas Nelson Publishers, 1998), p. 14.

Scripture Index

Subject Index

Other Books by
C. Peter Wagner

7 Power Principles
I Learned After *Seminary*

Freedom from the Religious Spirit
(C. Peter Wagner, General Editor)
Understanding How Deceptive Religious Forces Try to
Destroy God's Plan and Purpose for His Church

Changing Church
How God Is Leading His Church into the Future

Out of Africa
(C. Peter Wagner and Joseph Thompson, General Editors)
How the Spiritual Explosion Among Nigerians
Is Impacting the World

Churchquake!
How the New Apostolic Reformation Is Shaking Up
the Church as We Know It

Acts of the Holy Spirit
A Modern Commentary on the Book of Acts

Discover Your Spiritual Gifts
The Easy-to-Use Guide That Helps You Identify and Understand
Your Unique God-Given Spiritual Gifts

Your Spiritual Gifts Can Help Your Church Grow
The Best-Selling Guide for Discovering and Understanding Your
Unique Spiritual Gifts and Using Them to Bless Others

Breaking Strongholds in Your City
(C. Peter Wagner, General Editor)
How to Use Spiritual Mapping to Make Your Prayers
More Strategic, Effective and Targeted

The Prayer Shield
How to Intercede for Pastors, Christian Leaders and
Others on the Spiritual Frontlines

Faith Makes a Difference in the Workplace

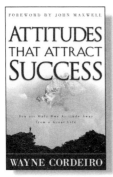

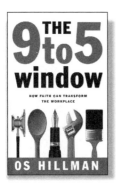
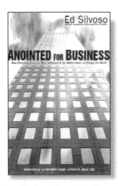
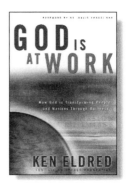

More of the Best from
C. Peter Wagner

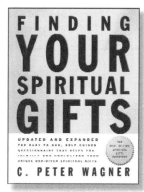

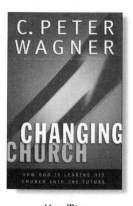

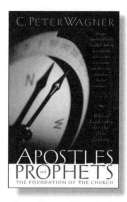